How to Survive an Ofsted Inspection

This book is d

ın Findlater

B L O O M S B U R Y
LONDON • NEW DELHI • NEW SHEFFIELD HALLAM UNIVERSITY

Bloomsbury Education
An imprint of Bloomsbury Publishing Plc

50 Bedford Square	1385 Broadway
London	New York
WC1B 3DP	NY 10018
UK	USA

www.bloomsbury.com

Bloomsbury is a registered trade mark of Bloomsbury Publishing Plc

Published 2015

© Sarah Findlater, 2015

Quotes from Ofsted documents used in this publication are approved under an Open Government Licence: www.nationalarchives.go.uk/doc/open-government-licence/

British Library Cataloguing-in-Publication Data
A catalogue record for this book is available from the British Library.

ISBN: PB: 9781472911063
ePub: 9781472911087
ePDF: 9781472911070

Library of Congress Cataloging-in-Publication Data
A catalog record for this book is available from the Library of Congress.

10 9 8 7 6 5 4 3 2 1

Typeset by Newgen Knowledge Works (P) Ltd., Chennai, India
Printed by CPI Group (UK) Ltd, Croydon, CR0 4YY

This book is produced using paper that is made from wood grown in managed, sustainable forests. It is natural, renewable and recyclable. The logging and manufacturing processes conform to the environmental regulations of the country of origin.

To view more of our titles please visit www.bloomsbury.com

Contents

Part 2 Around the corner 105

Part 3 Today's the day! 157

Part 4 Afterwards 193

Acknowledgements

I would like to dedicate this book to my wonderful husband. Without his unwavering support and belief in me I would be lost.

There are some very special teachers that I have had the pleasure of working with over the years that have taught me a great many lessons about myself as a professional and made me really think about my practice. Peg, Brian, Emma, Rhys, Ben, Marvin, Nita, Becky, Sophia, Donna, Leona, Mark, Tom, Jack, Nicola, Faye, Roisin and Rob thank you for being you.

A huge thank you goes out to all the dedicated teachers on Twitter who have been an inspiration to me in so many ways over the last couple of years. A special mention to Ross Morrison McGill who is a ray of sunshine on the darkest of days and has positively encouraged me from the outset.

Thank you to Sophie Bell for her primary school perspective input into the the the book. You are a star and your students are lucky to have you.

I would like to thank my father for his advice and guidance on this book and in my teaching career over the years. And my mother for her insatiable passion and drive that has been my inspiration and made me believe that anything is possible if you want it enough. (Including writing a whole book!). You two are great.

Online resources accompany this book at:
www.bloomsbury.com/survive-ofsted

Please type the URL into your web browser and follow the instructions to access the resources. If you experience any problems, please contact Bloomsbury at: companionwebsite@bloomsbury.com.

Introduction

School inspections are an unavoidable reality for all of us teachers. We need to make sure we are armed with the knowledge of what the inspection will involve so that there is no negative impact on our teaching and the student's learning when it happens. It is no good pulling out your bag of tricks and donning fancy dress as soon as the call from Ofsted comes in – we just need to be who we are and do that well. Knowing what will happen and what is expected of you over the course of the inspection will banish the mystery, take away some of the stress and ensure you can get yourself prepared and ready for an inspection any time. And that is what this book aims to do. That way, when the inspectors arrive, you can get on with what is important – teaching your classes and helping pupils learn the most that they can.

No one inspection is the same as the next so you cannot know every minute detail in advance, and you probably would not want to! Ofsted are now becoming much better at responding to feedback from teachers on the inspection process and are even altering their practice in line with this when appropriate. This means that inspections are not 'one-size-fits-all' and will differ from school to school – as they should. However the general guidance that inspectors follow are outlined below to help you understand what to expect.

What is an Ofsted inspection?

The independent government-regulated body Ofsted inspect providers across education, children's services and further education and skills (this book, however, focuses on how to survive an Ofsted inspection in primary and secondary schools only). School inspections are a legal requirement. An inspection can take place at any time in the academic year after five working school days of the Autumn term have passed. The team that visit your school will include a lead inspector and a number of associate inspectors. The headteacher or highest ranking senior leader will be contacted and informed of Ofsted's impending arrival. The inspection will normally take place over no more than two days. Before Ofsted arrive, they will have looked over your school's previous Ofsted report, performance data and any documents that have been provided to them via surveys or Parent View (Parent View is Ofsted's online parent questionnaire that is available for parents to fill in at any time on Ofsted's website: parentview.ofsted.gov.uk.) Findings from all of this data will form the inspection plan and help the inspection team know what to focus on during their time in school. However, the focus of the inspection may change if something crops up while they are on site that they wish to pursue further, positive or negative. Their aim throughout the inspection is to provide an independent external assessment of the quality and standards of education in the school. Once the inspection has taken place, the inspectors provide a report of their findings which becomes a public document, available for anyone to read online.

When are schools inspected?

A school can have anything up to five years between inspections but it can happen at any time if Ofsted have, or are alerted to any concerns. A school that is judged to be inadequate will be closely monitored and reinspected within 18 months of their last inspection. If a school is placed in special measures due to concerns noted in the inspection then it may receive up to five monitoring inspections during the 18 months following the initial inspection.

How much notice will the school be given before an inspection?

Depending on the individual provider and reason for the triggering of an inspection, there can be no notice whatsoever or one days notice.

What will happen during the inspection?

Inspectors will spend their time observing lessons and gathering first-hand evidence to help form their view of the school. They will look at the on-site and off-site provision provided for all pupils on roll, and they will look at the specific achievement of groups of pupils, including those eligible for Pupil Premium funding. As well as observing lessons they will hold discussions, both formally and informally, with staff and pupils, listen to pupils read and scrutinise their work and books. They will also look at a selection of school records and documents relating to pupils' achievement and safety.

How will staff be involved in the inspection?

The senior team in the school will be kept informed of what is happening in the inspection as it progresses. They will have the opportunity to clarify how any judgements are being made and provide additional evidence or documentation, where necessary, to inform the inspection. The headteacher will be invited to join the inspectors in a number of lesson observations. They will also be invited to attend the end of day inspection team meetings and comment on the inspection team's recommendations to ensure they are understood and accurate. Groups of staff such as NQTs or middle leaders may be invited to attend meetings with the inspection team to answer queries they may have about various things in the school.

What feedback is provided during or after the inspection?

Individual teachers whose teaching is observed will be offered some feedback at set times. This feedback will not involve any gradings, only strengths and possible areas for improvement. This may take place one-to-one or in groups. The senior leadership team (SLT) will be provided with the overall gradings for each category the school is judged under and be reminded that these gradings are subject to change. Once the inspection team has reached its conclusion, the judgements will be presented and explained to those responsible for governance of the school. The formal written report is usually provided to the school within ten working days and published on the Ofsted website within 15 working days. If the school is judged as inadequate then the report will be made available within 28 working days.

What do Ofsted judge during an inspection?

There are now (thankfully) a limited number of documents that Ofsted use to guide their inspection process. One of the key documents is the framework for school inspection which provides an overview of guidance on the school inspection process. In essence, it guides inspectors to focus on the aspects of a school's work that have, in Ofsted's opinion, the greatest impact on raising achievement. The inspectors form judgements on six key areas:

1. the achievement of pupils at the school
2. the quality of teaching in the school
3. the behaviour and safety of pupils at the school
4. the quality of leadership in and management of the school.

The additional two areas, if relevant to the school, are:

5. the early years provision
6. the post 16 provision.

Inspectors are also told that they must consider the provision for spiritual, moral, social and cultural (SMSC) development of the pupils, and the extent to which the school supports the needs of disabled pupils and those who have a special educational need (SEN) and those receiving Pupil Premium funding. It states that evidence must be collected from the headteacher, school staff, governors, parents and pupils of the school during the inspection. The general provision for early years or post 16 is judged for its effectiveness in terms of quality of education and standards.

What are the Ofsted gradings and how are they decided?

Another of the key documents provided by Ofsted is the school inspection handbook. This document is a detailed and lengthy breakdown of every aspect of the school inspection process and how the team form their judgements during the inspection. This document includes the descriptors for the grades awarded under each category Ofsted form a judgement on when they inspect: achievement, teaching, behaviour and safety, leadership, early years provision and post 16 provision. There are four grades available to each category:

- Grade 1: outstanding
- Grade 2: good
- Grade 3: requires improvement
- Grade 4: inadequate.

If a school is graded as inadequate and is considered to be a cause for concern then it will be placed in one of two categories: serious weakness or special measures.

The inspectors will gather, record and analyse the evidence they collect over the course of the inspection. The lead inspector will then discuss the findings and the team will form their collective judgements on each of the specified categories. The team will identify the strengths and areas for improvement of the school and what it must do to improve. The findings over the course of the inspection will be shared with the headteacher and relevant senior staff to allow them to provide additional evidence where relevant.

What should I look at if I am applying for a job at a school?

When going for interview at a new school they will be expecting you to have looked at and know the detail of their last Ofsted inspection. The Ofsted inspection report for any school can be found on the Ofsted website by searching the school name. Reading the report is a great way to see what strengths the school has so that you can look out for these and discuss them with the staff and students. The school will undoubtably have been working on the areas that were highlighted for improvement, so look out for things that highlight what they are doing in these areas on their website and in their prospectus. If you are already in the position of having secured a job at a new school then make sure that you are thinking of what you can offer to ensure that the school is moving forward with its areas for improvement. It takes everyone working together to form and maintain an outstanding school, so make sure you are doing your bit.

How will this book help me survive an inspection?

When the inspection call comes it can be easy to panic and not know where to begin to make sure you show off what happens in your classroom everyday and how outstanding everything is! This book is here to help you glide seamlessly through an inspection like it is any other day (well, as much as possible!).

This book aims to help you be as prepared as you possibly can be for the arrival of an Ofsted team at your school. You can read the book straight through from start to finish or dip into it as and when you need different sections. The book is divided into four parts, each corresponding to a different stage you may be at:

Part 1: Planning for the future: a guide to making your general practice the very best it can be long before Ofsted are even close to inspecting your school. Making your practice the best it can be and setting up systems and routines with your students, whether you are being inspected or not, is the best way to ensure you will excel when you are inspected.

Part 2: Around the corner: tips for when your school has received the call from Ofsted. This section focuses on your last minute preparations once you know Ofsted are on their way and you only have a short time to put those final touches in place to make you as cool, calm and collected as possible for the inspection. If needs must, this section will help you sort out what you can in a short space of time and can be used alone, but it is obviously even more effective if you have all of the guidance in place from the first section. Long term preparation is always better than doing it at the last minute!

Part 3: Today's the day!: advice to help you focus on what is important on the actual day of the inspection – to teach well.

Part 4: Afterwards: a final word to help you think about how best to help yourself and your school move on and become even better after the inspection.

All of the chapters in the book have practical advice and pick up and use ideas and activities, as well as guidance, to help you be the best you can for the Ofsted inspection, not only on the day but every day – day in, day out. The book covers all of the areas you need to consider and excel in to be prepared for an inspection.

Part 1 includes primary and secondary specific examples for making your practice the best it can be. The chapters in Part 1 and 2 also have a handy section called 'Inspection connection' that links the guidance and advice in the chapter to the relevant Ofsted inspection guidance documentation: either the school inspection handbook (www.gov. uk/government/publications/school-inspection-handbook) or the framework for school inspection (www.gov.uk/government/publications/ the-framework-for-school-inspection) – the full references can be found at the end of the book. Part 2 includes 'quick fix' sections for if Ofsted take you by surprise and there is an area of your practice you need some last minute help with, and 'going the extra mile' tips to really impress your visitors! Part 3 includes extracts from outstanding Ofsted reports so you can see the kind of thing Ofsted will write (full references also at the end of the book), with analysis of how you can be as outstanding as the school in the report! There are also 'remaining cool, calm and collected tips' to help you stay calm on the day. Part 4 includes 'looking to the future' boxes to help you make the most of Ofsted feedback.

This book is also accompanied by online resources which you can access here: www.bloomsbury.com/survive-ofsted. Here you will be able to find printable versions of the 'to do' and 'last checks' lists from part 2 and 3 respectively, as well as the additional resources listed at the end of the chapters in part 1.

If you have any questions feel free to tweet me: @MsFindlater. Don't forget to use the hashtag: #SurviveOfsted.

Happy reading!

Planning for the future

Overview

This section aims to give you practical tips on setting up systems and practices that will allow you to float through a future inspection with not a grey hair formed or a wrinkled brow in sight (well, almost). It is easy to get swept up in a sense of panic when the word 'Ofsted' is even mentioned in a school. This does not need to be the case. Ofsted should be a non-event or even a positive event if you have things in order. Planning and preparation with Ofsted in mind – but not *for* Ofsted – will lead to a relaxed and open approach when Ofsted comes a-knocking.

There is no magic pill or one way of doing things that leads to having a great inspection result. It is all about conscious choices, working together, honest reflection and making clear plans. Success is not one-size-fits-all; it comes in all shapes and sizes and so it should. My aim with this book is to suggest and help you find ways of doing things that will make your life easier and help you be happy with the teacher you are when Ofsted arrive. Ofsted or no Ofsted, I hope these tips can help you think about your practice and make improvements that you can be proud of.

Whether you are a primary or secondary teacher, I have focused on practical ideas that you can pick up today and use in your classroom tomorrow to see if they work for you. I highlight anything you need to be cautious of and suggest ways to develop your practice further if you so wish. There are some easy-to-use and adaptable resources available to go with ideas shared in each chapter. These are available to download from the online resources that accompany this book, and are listed for you at the end of each chapter. I have also included online and at the end of the book clear links to the key Ofsted inspection documents to save you the task of trawling the extensive documentation yourself.

I hope you find this section useful.

1
Vision

"Your vision will become clear only when you can look into your own heart. Who looks outside, dreams; who looks inside, awakens."

Carl Gustav Jung

When I applied to train as a teacher I thought long and hard about why I was applying, and looking over my application the passion I felt was clear. I had real direction and a clear vision as to why I wanted to be a teacher and what I wanted to achieve. As my training began, my focus on the WHY(?!) of doing that 'crazy job' slipped to the back of my mind as I frantically just got on with teaching. I learnt so much that year, but the only forward planning I undertook was how I was going to survive the next day without getting booed out of the room. That is how it had to be for me back then. With hindsight, what I wish I had done more of at the start was to step outside of my immediate experience and take in the bigger picture. That focus came back with time and some excellent training that showed me how to clarify my vision both as a classroom teacher and leader. It took me a while to reconnect with my original vision that had been so apparent when I took my first tentative steps into teaching; when I did, everything became clear and a real sense of pride in what I do now shines bright and constant.

Having a vision for your own practice is essential, even more so in this time of constant change in education. Whichever level we teach, we all feel the same pressures of changing goal posts, government interference and in-school demands. The only way you will remain relatively sane is if you have clear in your mind what your personal vision is as a teacher. Who do you want your students to be when they leave you? What kind of teacher do you want to be? What are your career aims? Having a clear vision as a foundation for your approach to teaching will ensure that you are moving towards being an outstanding teacher because you will be assured and clear about why you are doing what you are doing. Your lessons will be authentic and learning intentions will have a real purpose.

Putting it into practice

- **Your students:** Sit and form a collage or mind map – whichever you prefer – of all the things you would want the ideal student to be and what qualities you would desire to see in them by the time they leave you. You will be surprised how much this activity will make you think about your priorities in the classroom. If students were about to leave your classroom for the very last time, what would you want your impact to be on them and their lives? They are the reason you are here so plan for the end game. Form all of your lessons around this end goal, incorporating curriculum and assessment focuses as this makes for really high-quality lessons.

- **You as a teacher:** Forming a vision of the teacher you want to be and working towards that goal is not something that should stop once you finish your training. Reflecting on where you have been, where you are now and in which direction you are heading professionally is healthy. As teachers we should be continually learning about our subject or subjects and pedagogical issues to inform our teaching.

- **Your career:** Having direction certainly helps with focusing you in the here and now. Having a plan as to what you would like to achieve in your career is really important. You may have aspirations of being a headteacher, you may think that senior leadership looks hellish and want to remain in the classroom to be a master teacher, or you may be eager to lead your own department to glory. Whatever your career goals, make sure that you are always doing what you need to do in order to move in that direction – it makes for a happy life if you are steadily taking action, picking up projects and working towards your goals. It is also a great example to the students to see the progression staff make.

- **Your life:** There is no question about it; teaching is all-consuming. With this in mind it is really important to have a vision for your personal life too. Make sure you have goals that you are working towards outside of school life, in the real world. Share these with your students and colleagues; let them know there is more to you than just being a teacher (and remind yourself of this!). You don't need to tell everyone everything, but sharing a few extra-curricular achievements is a lovely way for students and staff to get to know you and feel connected with you a little more.

Inspection connection

In an inspection it will shine through if you have a clear vision for your teaching and your students. Having direction makes the learning focused and students feel secure, and this leads to you being able to show off great learning and good relationships. Ofsted want to see a love of learning and passion from both students and teachers alike, and having a clear vision you live by and that is well communicated to the students will aid this process. Students having a vision of what they want to be when they leave you will lead to a sense of purpose in their everyday approach to lessons and help them see the purpose of their learning.

The Ofsted outstanding criteria for teaching and learning talks about teachers having 'consistently high expectations of all pupils' and this is all about your vision. If everything you do in the classroom is to enable the students to get better then how can you go wrong?! Make it clear to the students regularly why you say and do the things you do: to get the very best out of them and be able to wave them off at the end of their time with you knowing that you have given them a great foundation for their next step in life.

Things to think about

- **In primary schools:** Think about the area you would like to move into and ensure that you take on the right projects or responsibility for a curriculum area early on to show off the best of your skills to the SLT.

- **In secondary schools:** With the ever-growing variety in the way secondary schools are organised there are lots of opportunities for you to develop. Make sure that each step you take is one that you have chosen and leads you in the right direction. Sometimes too much choice can lead you down an unwanted path.

Developing your practice

As mentioned, having a vision of what your next step is in your career or future is hugely beneficial. We are always talking to students about planning for their future and taking structured and clear steps towards those goals; are you doing this for yourself too? This does not just refer to your next career move – a future aspiration could be a step up into leadership, but it could also be working on a whole school project, organising an extra-curricular club that interests you, or perhaps a teaching and learning Continuing Professional Development (CPD) goal like improving your marking systems. Whatever you decide to focus on, it is important to develop yourself and reflect upon that process. Knowing what you want from your job will ensure you are satisfied and challenged throughout your role. Look at the CPD that is on offer around the areas or career steps you are interested in. A good place to start is the DfE teaching progression page: www.education.gov.uk/get-into-teaching/about-teaching/salary/progression.   Opportunities for development in teaching and learning are always changing so remember, Twitter and Google are your friends. Once you know what you want to progress in, ask to be trained. If you don't ask you don't get. If your boss knows what you want to achieve they can support you, if they don't they can't.

Note of caution

We will always have school-based constraints that we have to be mindful of and will have to adapt our practice to. Find a way to be you and work towards your vision while still working as a team with your school for the benefit of all students. Having a varied teaching team is a positive thing for a school and you need to find your way to fit in. If a school really does not fit you, find one that does to find happiness rather than being miserable and dragging others down with you. Everyone deserves happiness and there are so many different schools out there to choose from. If you know who you are professionally and are clear in expressing this then a school will know immediately if you are right and you should be able to tell if they are right for you.

Online resources

- What do I want my student to become? Reflection sheet
- What type of teacher do I want to be? Reflection sheet
- Career plotter

2

Systems and routines

"Rules help control the fun!"

Monica from *Friends*

I remember starting my career as a teacher and being overwhelmed by the sheer volume of work that is involved in a single day. Schools are so busy and there is so much going on that it is very easy for a teacher to get lost in it all. The lessons blur into one, marking mounts up to an unreasonable level, the plethora of characters you teach and your five (or sometimes more!) shows a day or the intensity of the same 30 faces and personalities from 9 till 3.30, leave you exhausted. I've been there. Small changes in the way I started to organise my day really helped me to start enjoying this great job I had managed to get, and not want to cry at the state of myself and my classroom at the end of the day!

Having strong and clear systems in place is the glue that holds everything together in a lesson. Students feel safe and secure when they know that their teacher has clear expectations, systems and routines in place and therefore are settled and ready to learn much more quickly. Systems make a teacher's life easier in every respect; they save time, focus students, improve behaviour, strengthen trust and allow teachers and students to take risks in teaching and learning. More importantly, they keep a teacher's sanity in tact! Get your systems and routines in place from the outset and keep the students well trained so that when the inspection arrives you will just have to do what you always do.

Putting it into practice

- **Entering the classroom:** Position yourself at the door at the start and end of lessons. This sends a clear message that you are cool, calm and collected and will not be flustered by the busyness of school life. If you collect your class from the playground at the start of the day, make sure that you have a quiet orderly line before entering the school to set the tone for the day ahead.

- **Exit from the classroom:** Keep an eye on the time during lessons or as break approaches by having a clock in a place that is easy to view. Ensure that you have enough time to close the lesson in an orderly manner. The learning needs to be clarified and evaluated for students to leave knowing that they have achieved. Having a regular routine such as standing silently behind chairs after having cleared their tables is useful. Once the routine is in place you don't need to waste time telling them to do this; they just will. I always like to thank them for their work and wish them a good day as they leave one table at a time. Leaving in groups rather than en masse allows you the time and space to personally see each student off and deal with any issues you wish to. Insisting that there is a standard of behaviour at the end of the lesson or during transitions for the primary classroom, states the tone for your next lesson.

- **Student monitors:** Allocate monitoring jobs to the students on rotation. Give them responsibility for, for example, handing the books out, opening or closing blinds, highlighting key words throughout the lesson, choosing the best answer given in the lesson, spotting when the learning objective is being addressed by students feeding back or handing out equipment. This not only saves you time but makes the lesson run more smoothly. Make sure you reward them with a certificate or badge at the end of a stint as a monitor.

- **Attendance:** Making sure you are keeping up to date with school expectations of marking attendance is an easy routine to set in place. You could use the taking of the register as an opportunity to greet each student individually, collect in homework, revise previous learning or as part of the starter. For those who only take the register once or twice a day, you could use it to test learning from the previous afternoon at morning registration or what they have remembered from the morning lessons at afternoon registration. How about making up a fun story and including their names as you go to keep them interested and on their toes to answer their name when it crops up in the story. Makes taking the register fun!

- **Group work:** Having routines for group work is a must. Unstructured group work with young people can be a hideous waste of time if there are no routines and students are not trained in how to do it effectively. Clear expectations need to be set out and students reminded of expectations regularly. Roles allocated within groups such as researcher, scribe and devil's advocate are always a great way to keep things focused. In primary school, giving the students stickers or badges to wear with their job titles will keep them focused and allow supporting adults to easily check each person is sticking to their role. Have a laminate with your group work rules on in an easily accessible place so students can pick it up to remind them of good group work practice.

- **Marking and feedback:** There will be a marking and feedback policy that your school insists upon and you should ensure that you are following this. However, within these boundaries you need to also find a way to make marking and feedback work for you and your particular students. There is no one-size-fits-all approach. Systems that are helpful include: using codes for regularly used targets and getting students to write out the targets by identifying the code; marking a set amount of books each day over the course of two weeks on rotation (this particularly helps secondary teachers ensure they keep up without taking 120 books home just before a marking deadline!); training students to effectively peer mark using the mark scheme that you use so that you can have either them or you mark work in books. Primary children can also be taught to mark their own work against a success criteria that you have created – get them to highlight sections against the success criteria to show you the skills they have used, allowing for quick marking.

- **Class tasks:** Having a clear starting point, time frame and end point to tasks ensures that all students are focused and keeps the pace of the lesson at an appropriate level. Finding key phrases that you like to use at different points in the lesson is always fun and can be reassuring and motivational for students. Phrases to start off tasks could include: 'ready, set, go … ', 'eyes down, minds on the task' and 'let's get going' or 'and we're off!'. To keep them on task, you could: read out examples of good work as you circulate, specifically praise those who are displaying excellent focus or working well, alert them to time left or specify where they should be within the task at certain points. For younger children it can be helpful to have a timer on the interactive whiteboard displaying how long they have left on a task. The more you use these strategies and mix them up the more impact this will have.

- **Getting students' attention:** There are many routines you can put in place to get students' attention in a lesson; which one you employ will depend on you as a person, the class and the type of activity you are doing in the lesson. The last thing you want to do is to fall into the dreaded 'shhhhh', as your class ignore you because they hear it so often! The way to avoid this trap is to set up routines that allow you to get their attention in a less mundane manner. You will need to explain these techniques to your students and train them in what they should do to ensure that they respond to them. You could try standing at a central point in the class and raising your arm; having asked all students to raise their hand, face the front and be silent when they see you or another student raising their arm, and wait silently until they are focused and facing you. Clap a rhythm that all students must then emulate and clap in response to you, followed by them facing you silently. Count up and challenge them to be silent and facing you as soon as possible when they hear you counting; make it into a game. Count down from five making it a requirement to be silent and facing you when you get to zero. Alternatively, you could have some wind chimes or bells in a fixed point in the room and gently chime them until you get the students' attention.

- **Asking for help:** Having clear routines that students are aware of when they need help avoids students using 'not understanding' as an excuse not to work. For secondary students, have a help point in the class including revision materials, key word laminates, literacy aids, computer access and other tools to assist them, and encourage them to use it independently to search for answers. Encourage them to use their peers before you; the 'ask three before me' rule is a good one to follow. For younger children, the four Bs works nicely: Brain – think about what you need to do; Book – access any resources in the room you need to help you; Buddy – ask another child; Boss – ask one of the adults.

- **Reward system:** Rewards are often far more powerful than sanctions. By that I don't necessarily mean money or actual prizes, although I know many schools do this and it can be effective at times. Rewards I love using with students include merits or house points, certificates, publicly appreciating or celebrating, badges or pins and phone calls or letters home. In addition in a primary setting, you could add examples of good work to your working wall, send children to share their work with senior staff, show work to parents at the end of the day or add work to your class blog. Celebrate your student's successes. When they do well they deserve it! Don't let these routines fade as the year or term goes on. If you remain consistent with rewards students will remain responsive to them.

- **Behaviour system:** Ensure that from the outset you make clear your expectations of students' behaviour and reinforce these expectations every lesson. It is a good idea to have your rules displayed in the room somewhere as a reminder. Don't let things go or you will lose the faith of all your students and behaviour will worsen. If you have let this slip you will have to work hard to regain them, but it is very doable so don't give up and remain strong. Be mindful though, you would not want your main focus on the walls to be behaviour sanctions – a small poster will do.

Inspection connection

Ofsted inspectors are guided to look into and observe the use of the 'systems of the school' so make sure you know your whole school policies well and are following them day in, day out. There will be times when you are not in complete agreement with every iota of a policy so make sure you have discussed this in private with your line manager when your concerns are first felt so that you can find a way to work within the system and ensure you are a team player.

The Ofsted outstanding criteria for teaching highlights a need for teachers to 'systematically and effectively check pupils' understanding throughout lessons, anticipating where they may need to intervene and doing so with notable impact on the quality of learning.' Having routines in class that you use all the time to make sure students are on track, and having interventions ready to boost those that need it will make everything run smoothly day-to-day. Then when it comes to the inspection day you just need to do what you always do and job done.

The Ofsted outstanding criteria for leadership and management talks about 'the establishment of an orderly and hardworking school community' and this requires well thought out and clear systems in place around the school but also in every classroom. Yes the senior leadership team are responsible for ensuring these systems are being followed but we are all leaders in our own classroom so we need to make sure we do our bit to make this a reality. Clear routines and systems that the pupils expect to follow in the same way as around the school builds trust and allows students to focus on what is important – learning.

Things to think about

The layout of your classroom needs to be taken into consideration when setting up routines and systems. Make sure you have the classroom set up in a way that will allow for the routines and systems to be carried out without unnecessary fuss.

- **In primary schools:** Having the same class for a longer period of time enables you to hone your systems and get the students working with you quite quickly. Train them in as many routines as possible. For example: always be in the playground a few minutes before the start of school so you are available to parents without them delaying your progress into school; make sure the children know any letters or notes will be collected and dealt with once you are inside the classroom.
- **In secondary schools:** As you will see lots of students, but not necessarily everyday, you need to ensure you are being consistent and really work on the systems at the start. Once they are in place your life in school will be so much easier. Having common systems that you use with all classes is a must to avoid confusion for you and the students. You may want to have a couple of different systems for particular groups, depending on their needs.

Developing your practice

You should always set the tone in the first instance but once that is done you could involve the students in devising new routines and systems for the class. Giving them a little ownership in shaping the classroom atmosphere can be a powerful experience for all involved.

Note of caution

We all have whole school systems in place that need to be adhered to. If we don't then we are building distrust in the school and this will be detrimental to the students in the long-run. They need us united as teachers. Your systems don't need to be identical to every other teacher's but they should be in line with the whole school policy for the sake of the students.

Online resources

- Student monitors poster
- Group work roles handout
- Marking codes handout
- Help desk poster
- Three before me poster

3

Seating plan

"Find your seating arrangement here but your place is on the dance floor!"
Wedding sign

One system you should have in place in your classroom is your plan for seating. Over the years I have experimented with many classroom seating plans. They all have their benefits. The first classroom I taught in had computers all around the outside taking up lots of space with limited space for me to work within. I had to have the tables in rows to fit them all in. This worked well for individual focused work and keeping the noise down which helped me as an inexperienced teacher! The second classroom I taught in was larger and allowed for grouped tables of four. I stuck with the groups of four in my third classroom as I liked the dynamic. Groups of four are a good size as the groups are not too large for each student to contribute in any activity and not too distracting to allow for quiet, focused individual work. Following this I was classroom-less and in a state of constant movement. Having to use lots of different rooms really opened my eyes to the difference seating and classroom arrangement can make. At the moment I have groups of six for the first time (initially due to the fact that groups of four did not fit the room) and have found this really easy to manage and great for debate and collaboration.

There is no right way to seat students. You need to find a way that works for you and the students and allows for the best learning environment for everyone. However you choose to organise them, ensure that you have planned well and indicated on a seating or lesson plan the reasons behind your choice. Don't just stick to the same routine; experiment with different seating with different groups and activities more than once and really reflect on the benefits of each set-up – you may be surprised at what you find.

Putting it into practice

- **Ability**: It is always a good idea to keep ability and students' specific needs in mind when arranging your seating. Grouping students of similar ability can help with differentiation of resource, questioning and task. When buddying up lower and higher ability students you can still keep the challenge high by getting the higher ability students to lead the task. Allowing students to act as teachers to one another benefits both lower and higher ability students.

- **Groups**: Grouped tables are great for ease of switching focus and activity type without much fuss. Groups of four are generally better than six as it encourages all students to take part in a group task. Another benefit of grouping students is that you can easily bring in an element of healthy competition. Grouped tables can encourage off task talking though, so make sure you keep on top of that.

- **Rows**: Tables arranged in rows work well for focused teacher-led lessons or extended individual quiet working environments. This is obviously not always appropriate, so having rows that are formed of two tables of two together can aid possible group work. Be mindful of ensuring that you can access all students in the room. There needs to be enough space between each row for you to move between them. Consider whether you want straight rows or angled ones aimed towards the focus point in the room.

- **Horseshoe**: The horseshoe has the benefit of allowing for a feeling of togetherness in the classroom. Whole class discussion is a very different experience as all students can see and interact with one another. You can mix up the traditional horse shoe arrangement and have a central table for targeted intervention groups or have a number of tables of two branching off the horseshoe to enable a less circular arrangement. Students will have to move chairs and tables for group work.

- **Pairs**: Tables of two all facing the front is a very traditional set-up and not seen as often as it once was. Not many classrooms are big enough to cater for this arrangement now. Pairs can be arranged to face the front or at an angle. Grouped work can be completed fairly easily as they can turn to face another pair in the class.

Inspection connection

Ofsted consider how 'effectively pupils are grouped within lessons' when they are conducting the inspection. It is vital that whatever your seating plan is within the classroom there is a clear logic behind the set-up and that it is reviewed for effectiveness regularly. If one way is not working then change it and make it work. You could make sure that you have a seating plan with a brief description of the theory behind the plan for the inspector to glance at when they pop in. Sometimes what is obvious to you may need to be clearly explained for an observer.

Ofsted specifically mention considering 'whether the most able are stretched and the least able are supported sufficiently to meet their full potential' in mixed ability groups and classes. Make sure that when you are organising your seating you are thinking about how it will impact on students of differing abilities. Does the seating enable all students to get what they need from the lesson? If not, what can you do to alter this outcome?

That being said, this will look different in every classroom because Ofsted clearly state that they do not advocate a 'preferred methodology' and this applies to seating as well as teaching and assessment in your classroom. Do what works for your students and share the theory behind your decisions. Be mindful to focus on the student outcomes and not your personal preference.

Things to think about

There will always be some arrangements that just will not work in the space you have. Consider the arrangement carefully to allow for free flow around the room. You need to be able to get to every student with ease for the arrangement to work well. Ensure that no student is facing away from the board as this will make for an uncomfortable lesson experience for that unlucky student and could lead to disruptive behaviour.

- **In primary schools:** Have very specific seating for literacy and numeracy based on the knowledge you have of your students and their learning needs.
- **In secondary schools:** Try thinking about a seating arrangement that you can just slightly alter to change the feel of the room rather than having to shift the whole lot and interrupt what is already a short time with the class.

Developing your practice

There may be a number of arrangements you like to use for different tasks. Try having seating plans for a number of classroom arrangements that the students are all aware of. I often print off the seating plans and have them displayed somewhere in the room for ease of access. Get the students to move the classroom furniture around as and when needed.

Note of caution

Make sure that you choose the seating that works for the students as well as you. Try to avoid using seating as a behaviour tool. Students should behave because you have clear rules and expectations of them, not because of furniture arrangement. Deal with the behaviours, don't mask them because they will always rear their ugly heads at some point. Consider personalities when making a seating plan but be careful to not always place 'good' children next to those with behavioural issues as it can be very wearing for them to be used as a natural barrier.

Online resources

- Seating plan template: groups of four
- Seating plan template: groups of six
- Seating plan template: rows
- Seating plan template: horseshoe
- Seating plan template: pairs

4

Classroom set-up

"Almost all quality improvement comes via simplification of design, manufacturing … layout, processes and procedures."

Tom Peters

When I became head of faculty, one of my first big challenges was the learning environment. I remember walking around the English, MFL and media department rooms with an HMI inspector that was in for the day to give me feedback on my progress so far with the team. As we walked around I was telling him all the wonderful things my team had achieved in the last year and how proud we all were. He was suitably impressed, but as we wondered around there was one glaringly obvious thing that was bringing us down still … the state of the classrooms. There was lots of excess furniture, unloved messy corners, peeling paint, crowded classrooms and dated displays. It was obvious when he pointed it out but when you work in the same rooms day in, day out you can become blind to the surroundings.

The choices you make when laying out your classroom can have a real impact on the way students approach your lessons. People take such care over the arrangement and design of their own homes because they feel it is important. Yet when it comes to the classroom (a place in which teachers spend a large amount of their day in) they often don't consider it even half as much. Well, we should because it makes a difference.

Putting it into practice

- **Shelving**: Having adequate shelving in a classroom is essential. Make sure you have trays or boxes if you can, to hold books for different lessons that can very easily be taken out and put away to save time and keep everything well ordered. Have shelves with books on them in a place that is accessible for students so that you don't have to do all the lugging about in lessons. Make sure all shelves and trays/boxes are clearly labelled and have an allocated place – the school day is busy and you don't want to be spending the end of every day sorting out an unholy mess.

- **Tables**: When setting up your tables, whatever your choice of layout, make sure that you have imagined the class full of students sitting in their seats and how much space that will take up. You need to have an easy flow around the classroom so that you can access all students easily and quickly. Having to constantly move a student to get past them or not being able to go to a certain area of the classroom quickly lends itself to behaviour management problems and some students not being assisted as often.

- **Blinds:** This may sound silly but making sure the right blinds/ curtains are in place in the classroom is so important. I can't tell you how many times I have been in classrooms that have insufficient blinds and glaring sun streams on to the interactive whiteboard for a good section of the day. This can really ruin the impact of a lesson if you are using the interactive whiteboard to introduce or inspire. Fight hard for the right blinds, especially if it impacts on learning or shines right in a pupil's eyeline as they are working.

- **Displays:** Ensure that displays are clear, bright and useful. Moreover, ensure that they are in a place that students can see and use them, but not in a place where they will become damaged easily; you will have very messy walls or spend your life replacing them.

- **Resources:** Have a 'stretch and challenge' task box in a set place within your room with tasks that could apply to any topic being studied. If at any time a student has completed all of the work to a high standard before the other students, they will never be left without an opportunity to learn more. Consider having essential resources in the centre of tables for students to use and place back again at the end of the lesson to avoid always spending time handing or sorting them out.

- **Surfaces**: How about trying out some half whiteboard, half desk tables? There are some great products out there that are very easy to use and can transform a boring, plain school desk into a multi-use tool. There are whiteboard strips of plastic that come on a roll and can just be rolled out and stuck on. There is also a very handy paint available that can be used on any surface to turn it instantly into a whiteboard. No need for getting the mini whiteboards in and out of the resources cupboard anymore – they are right there in front of the students.

Inspection connection

Ofsted will look at the degree of respect students show 'for the school's learning environments … facilities and equipment.' If you have taken time and care in setting up your classroom and keep it orderly then students will automatically do the same – you create the culture in your classroom. Have high standards for your space and demand this of the students too. It makes for a nicer place to be and learn. Don't allow pens to be lost, bags to be strewn across the floor, equipment to be misused or learning spaces to be left messy from day one and there will be no battle to be won in this area – they will just be in the habit.

Things to think about

- **In primary schools:** Ensure you have the numeracy and literacy displays in an easily accessible place in the room as they will need to be updated regularly. Working walls should be at the front of the room, where you do most of your teaching and easy for all the class to see. Also, if you are lucky enough to have computers in your room, make sure you have them facing you rather than the wall so that you can easily keep an eye on the screens when students are working on them. Try zoning out your classroom in a physical and visual sense so that students can easily get into an activity you do regularly like reading or role-play. Teach your children how to move the furniture safely so they can help you quickly and easily to rearrange your room and put it back again. Lessons like philosophy benefit from students being sat in a horseshoe.

- **In secondary schools:** As you will have many different year groups coming in and out of your lessons, make sure that you have organised your resources and where you store them with this in mind. Remember that some classes are bigger than others and the space needs to work for all of them without hassle.

Developing your practice

Consider involving students in the decision-making when it comes to the organisation of the room. You could give them a couple of possible arrangements and then take a vote. Getting the students' perspective can bring up some surprising considerations that otherwise would not necessarily have been thought of.

Note of caution

Always think about practicality above all else. If it looks nice in the room but is not practical then it is likely to be a distraction and a source of disruption. Ensure that when you are organising the room you think of it at its busiest and how it would work at that point in the day. If it won't work then change the set-up.

Online resources

- Drawer/shelf labels template
- Room organisation template
- Student classroom set-up survey

5
Displays

"You can feel the love in a classroom when you walk in and the walls have interesting stuff on them. You know the teachers who care and the teachers who don't from their walls I reckon."

Year 10 student

I remember that feeling of walking into my very first classroom a few days before the end of the summer holidays. I arrived armed with a staple gun and a bag full of bits and bobs to help me make that room a place that the students and I really wanted to be. Staring at the peeling paint, ten years worth of display backing layers on each display board and the amount of wall space I had to sort out, I wondered if it was worth the time and effort to sort it all out. I put some music on and danced around my classroom all day slowly adding colour and inspirations to every wall space I could in the room. The final result was great and I have done that to every class I have worked in since. The effort is well worth it and the students treat the room differently if they see that you care about it too.

Whatever your classroom is like when you arrive, make it yours and your lessons will feel the impact. There is nothing worse than an unloved classroom, faded posters and messy displays. A lick of paint and some simple and colourful pieces up on the wall can transform the room into a learning hub that any student would look forward to coming into. You can really create a mood by how the classroom is decorated and what the displays depict. The students will judge you by the room. Do you want to be messy, unloved and disorganised, or bright, clear and essential reading? Get your displays up to scratch now and then you'll only have to spruce them up on come the day of the inspection!

Putting it into practice

- **Student work treasure box:** Make sure you save up/scan/ photocopy/take a photo of great examples as you mark work. You could have a treasure box with these pieces stored in it to pick out when the displays are looking a little tired and put up on the wall. It is lovely to have clean and clear pieces just for show occasionally, but neat and readable marking on the work is also great so that students can see your workings for when you are marking their work in the future.

- **Subject-specific displays:** It is always good to have some subject-specific display areas in your room that will remain largely static. These may change simply to refresh the colours or ensure they are still attractive to the eye. Assessment criteria, exam breakdowns, topics covered over the year, inspirational quotes about your subject/s, images for inspiration, key words, etc. These are essential for the walls but make sure you make them readable, colourful and accessible for all students so that it is not just wallpaper. Use the displays regularly in your lessons so that students are trained and used to going up and checking for information on the walls. It may sound obvious to include this on your walls, but I have seen so many unloved classrooms that I cannot ignore it. It really does make a difference.

- **Literacy:** No matter what phase or subject we teach, literacy will always be central to our subject. Literacy displays can be as simple as key words and their definitions up around the room. You could create a fun display with the essential ideas to consider in terms of spelling, punctuation and grammar in your subject. Ensuring that literacy is seen as important in your classroom can very easily be backed up by simple and friendly displays. Once again, use them as you teach, refer to them and refer your students to them if they need literacy tips or advice.

- **Colours:** There have been many studies into the impact colour can have in the classroom, and there are many different views on the matter. General colour advice tends to be that blue, green or yellow can have positive effects on learning and concentration. Whatever you believe, make sure you have some variety in the room either through actual wall colours or the displays themselves. A variety of colours in the room will make it inviting and exciting to be in. A dull room creates a dull mood.

- **Sections:** Try creating sections within the classroom through display – have sections that explore certain subjects, inspirational quotes, literacy or 'what can I do with this subject in my future?'. Having information displayed in your room in order and flowing well from one section to another will keep the students interested and allow them to easily find what they need on the walls.

Inspection connection

Ofsted take into consideration what they witness in terms of the 'pupils' respect for the school's learning environment' in and around the school. This will include the displays in and around your classroom and department. If the students have clearly contributed to displays, and their work is being celebrated, then they will automatically have a higher respect for their surroundings as they have an investment in it. Actions speak louder than words, and the surroundings are a reflection of the actions of teachers and students in that space. Make the displays represent the great learning that goes on in your classroom and the students will beam with pride and respect.

Things to think about

- **In primary schools:** Having your own room where students learn a wide variety of topics in the same space lends itself to having great displays supporting learning and sectioning out the room. Displays can have a range of purposes: to celebrate achievement and show off children's best work, track progress, support and inspire. Working walls are a great way to focus students on a final outcome and track the skills they have learnt on the way. At the beginning of a unit of work write the unit's objective on the working wall and throughout the unit add resources, ideas and good examples of work for students to refer to. Working walls don't need to be neat, but they do need to be accessible. They should be quick and easy to create by just pinning and sticking as you go. For younger children, create interactive displays on walls and surfaces, display work on washing lines across the classroom, and get down to their level to view your displays from their perspective. Primary schools are very seasonal places but be aware that seasonal displays will have to be changed promptly.

- **In secondary schools:** Don't lose the fun just because you are teaching older students. Students of all ages need inspiration and a place they want to be to learn effectively. Don't presume that it is 'a primary thing' to have bright, interesting and fun displays for learning. Keep the love of learning alive by creating a space where students walk in and learn even before you are teaching them.

Developing your practice

Get the students voting on what the next display will include; give them some options on topic, colour, images, font etc. Involving students in this thought process means the displays are more likely to have the desired impact.

Note of caution

Make sure that you don't just put things on the wall to fill space. If the walls are overcrowded and messy, students will not pay attention to the displays or notice new content. The keys to a good classroom display are that displays are clear, useful and interesting to look at. Everything on the walls should be of some use or inspiration to the students.

Online resources

- Classroom display plan
- Classroom sign template
- Colour considerations

6
Teaching style

"It's a new era in fashion – there are no rules. It is all about the individual and personal style, wearing high-end, low-end, classic labels, and up-and-coming designers all together."

Alexander McQueen

Over the years I have changed as a teacher. This is not a mindful change or a move away from the 'real me' to the 'teacher me'. I have developed as a person as I have gained experience in school and this has naturally shone through in my approach in the classroom. As the years have passed I have become more myself in the classroom than ever. For me that was important as I felt that my life was too disjointed as a teacher and a person. I am a firm advocate of keeping personal and professional very separate, but not personality and professionalism. Personality shining through in the classroom is so important for a teacher. We are all different and this should be celebrated. Some teachers are active and animated while others are more calm and steady in the classroom. Both can work and students should have a mixed diet of people in school as they will in life. I became comfortable with being me and being professional all in one; it makes for a happier life.

It is important that teachers reflect on themselves as people and how others may see them. If you don't do this then the students will do it for you. Know and love your professional self; good and bad. Students have a natural curiosity and interest in their teachers so just make sure you are comfortable with who you are and remain true to this. You don't need to share the finer details of your personal life with students to ensure that they know and feel a connection with you. Remember, Ofsted does not advocate any one style or approach to teaching and learning. Do what you know works for your students in your setting.

Putting it into practice

- **Originality:** We are all one of a kind and this should be celebrated in the classroom. Make sure you bring this originality into your everyday teaching. Students look to their teachers to see what is acceptable and 'normal', whether they admit it or not. Whilst we need to make sure they fall in line and follow school rules, just as they will have to follow rules in the adult world once they leave school, it is also our place to ensure that they know that being different is not a bad thing – it is what makes the world such a wonderful place. If you are proud of who you are, it is a step in the right direction for students to love themselves for who they are. Learning to appreciate and celebrate people (teachers and students) for who they are, even if they are different, is one of those not-in-the-National-Curriculum lessons that we are all teaching all of the time and there is no getting away from that.

- **Anecdotes:** If you can bring in a few anecdotes from your own life it can really bring a topic to life for students; obviously only ones you feel comfortable sharing and that are appropriate to the topic. Students' ears prick up and eyes sparkle a little when you talk about real life. It can bring the subject alive for them and make them see the connections with what they are taught and where that may lead them later in life. We all crave human connection and our students are no different. Make your teaching style about you and who you are as well as the subject you are teaching.

- **Consistency:** Although it is important to bring your personality into the classroom and be yourself, we must always remember that we are professionals. Your emotions need to be stable and consistent in the classroom for you to be doing the best for the students. We must all leave our issues at the door and pick them up when we leave. The classroom is no place for adult emotional reactions. We work with children, they will try to push our buttons because that is what children do – be prepared for that. Calm, regal and reasoned at all times is essential for success. It is not easy but it is essential.

- **Out-and-about:** What the students, and staff for that matter, think of you as a teacher is formed both inside and outside the classroom. Making sure that you get out and about and see the students outside the classroom is a great way to get to know them better. Go and join in with their football or table tennis game and have a little fun with them. Get out and give them a cheer when they are playing sport against another school; the support will be well received. Have a wander around the playground at break or lunch and speak to the students. It may seem like there is no time to do this, but it really does have an impact and is worth making time for; teaching is all about relationships and this is a great way to cement them. It is a good idea to get some fresh air anyway as we do tend to be in at the crack of dawn and leave late so fresh air is not a regular in our day – give yourselves a break from the stuffy school building air.

- **Perception and reality:** Sometimes what we think we are like as a teacher is actually not the reality to everyone else. It is important to keep it real when it comes to what you are putting out there. Whenever I have done a 360 degree review of myself, I have grown as a person; some of the feedback was a surprise to me but it really made me think. Make sure you are not deluded about what the staff and students experience from you as a teacher, and that you are happy with what you are like and how you make others feel.

- **Element of surprise:** Sometimes it is fun to completely turn your teaching style on its head and surprise the students with a lesson or activity they would not normally expect from you. It keeps things fun and fresh in the classroom and gets the students talking too; they often like to reminisce about lessons or events that were unusual in school. Doing something different and talking with the students about it helps them see that you can take a risk and work outside your comfort zone, which in turn encourages them to do so in their work too.

Inspection connection

Ofsted clearly state that they do 'not favour any particular teaching style' and this is very important. What this means is that differences are celebrated and that we are not expected to be robots all fitting a certain mould. However we must be mindful that our teaching style needs to be for the benefit of the students, not just because that is how we are and we don't want to change.

Ofsted emphasise that it is up to the school leaders and teachers to decide for themselves how best to teach the students they have in their school. They talk of giving an 'opportunity, through questioning by inspectors, to explain why they have made the decisions they have and provide evidence of the effectiveness of their choices.' No longer will they be looking specifically for particular activities or teaching approaches but focusing more on what is working well. They mention looking at the 'impact of the quality and challenge of the work set.' This is empowering for sure. It is also a clear responsibility of the teacher and SLT to ensure that the best approaches for their particular students are being employed. Tracking and monitoring of progress, coupled with interventions and adaptations to practice, is essential for us to know for sure we are doing what works for the students.

Things to think about

- **In primary schools:** With a lot of effort and consistency at the start of the year, you will be free to be yourself with the students as they will be used to your routines and style. Have fun with them and enjoy the bonding time that follows getting everything running as you would like. Share something you love with your class. If you have golden time, offer to teach them something away from the curriculum. Teach them a craft or skill you enjoy or pick a new one to learn alongside them. Young children have no qualms in asking adults very personal questions. Have some answers ready up your sleeve or flip it round and tell them it is an interesting question and ask them why they want to know.

- **In secondary schools:** Teenagers have a tendency to become attached to certain teachers at different stages as they grow up. Be mindful that you need to care for them and support them, but keep a healthy distance so they do not come to over rely on you – you are not their friend, you are their teacher and lines can blur very quickly for teens. Be you, but be clear that there is a line they do not cross, then everyone is happy.

Developing your practice

Reflect on yourself professionally on a regular basis to ensure you remain happy with your growth as a teacher and the experience your students are getting. Don't beat yourself up, you are never going to please everyone, but make sure that you are happy with what you put out there and how it is perceived. Be honest with yourself and improve on what you don't like.

Note of caution

Be mindful of oversharing. Students do not need to know details of your personal woes to know you as a teacher. There is a line that should not be crossed and this line should be clear from the outset. Save offloading for friends and line managers behind closed doors.

Online resources

- Teaching style reflection worksheet
- 360 degree review questionnaire

7

Working as a team

"Talent wins games, but teamwork and intelligence wins championships."
Michael Jordan

A fractured team in a school can have devastating repercussions for staff and students alike. I have coached a number of colleagues over the years who have led teams in trouble: one colleague had a team that included a teacher who was very effective in the classroom but who was causing havoc outside the classroom by blocking change, spreading rumours, speaking unprofessionally to students about other teachers and making life difficult for others in the team. It can be a really horrid experience working in a team where someone is acting in this manner. Another colleague had the classic 'lone ranger' in their team: a teacher who is great in their own classroom, but not a part of the school community or team they work within.

As teachers we are in school to do a very important job, and if different people are pulling in opposite directions it can make life really difficult, so it is really important that you think about how you yourself can work as a really effective member of your school team.

As well as thinking about your own behaviours, in order to be able to work well as a team with every member of staff in your school it is so important to foster great relationships with as many people as possible, whatever their job role. One thing that is glaringly obvious and cannot be hidden away when a visitor comes to the school, be it Ofsted or anyone else, is the mood of the school. Adults set the tone for this mood and the students very quickly then reflect it. If there is animosity and negativity then this is likely to set the tone of the school and rub off on the students. If there is harmony and a sense of comradeship then this too will be apparent in the way students interact. We all need to ensure that we are creating a school where adults and children want to be, and that comes from the input of every one of us. The school community spans from the front of house staff who greet you as you arrive to the site staff that clear the playground at the end of break. We are all in it together and if that attitude is prevalent in your school then it will be clear.

At times, school is a lonely place. Everyone is so busy – students and staff alike – that it is quite easy to feel isolated. Starting a new job is often a very daunting process and it is natural at this time to feel a sense of being alone, but it is not necessarily the only time; seasoned teachers can also feel lonely. There are so many changes in education that all of us can feel lost – new staff, new students, new initiatives, new educational news stories, new curriculum – so much is new all the time! We have a duty to buoy one another along whatever our role in school. It makes for a happier teacher if the school workforce is united. We are all cogs in a wild and wonderful machine and the way we work together most definitely affects the articles we produce – our students. It is also a really invaluable lesson for students to see teachers working together and supporting one another regardless of what our actual position is within the school structure.

Putting it into practice

- **Team player:** Whatever your personal thoughts are about the teacher at the other end of the corridor, make sure that professionally you are supportive for the sake of your team. You can work well with someone who is your exact opposite and really gain from one another; we are losing out if we just share our professional time with those that we are naturally drawn to. Appreciate everyone for the different things they can bring to the table. A great activity to do with your team is the Myers-Briggs personality test which really gets you thinking about what you can contribute and what your needs really are, as opposed to what you think they are – the results were surprising for me.
- **Caring:** Part of being a good team is ensuring that you care for one another. The pace of the school day can mean we overlook

when someone is really struggling. We do a challenging job and sometimes we just need someone to stop for a minute in the hallways and check if we are okay and smile. It makes me sad when teachers storm towards the photocopy room/classroom/dinner hall eyes down and oblivious to anything else – wake up and live in the now. Appreciate others around you and they will do the same when you are having a rough day.

- **Your strengths:** Knowing what you are actually good at really helps you develop yourself as a professional. It may be that you are particularly good at questioning, having great starters or plenaries, dealing with difficult students, using educational technology, or creating tasks that build knowledge and skills through a lesson. Whatever you do well, it is your duty to share this with your team and it is their duty to do the same in return. So many teachers are coy about what they do well but there is no need. You could help others develop and help yourself in weaker areas – get shouting about your talents!

- **Other's strengths:** Sometimes it is down to others to praise brilliant practitioners. If you know that another teacher does something well, or have heard students talk about something great that they did in another teacher's lesson, then tell them about it and tell others about it. Singing one another's praises when they are due is a real team morale booster. Don't wait for formal observations or for a member of the SLT to spot something – step in and work as a team to appreciate one another and learn what we can grab from each other. Many hands make light work.

- **Negativity:** Avoid the mood hoovers! Don't give people who try and drag the team down any airtime. It is easy to be negative in a high-pressured and fast-paced environment, but resist it. Surround yourself with positivity like an armour. We need to be strong and united to face what we do everyday and negativity will only weaken you and bring you down. You do not have to be blind to issues, but approach them with a solution rather than just repeatedly stating the problems. If you really can't stand the school you are in then you must move – there are plenty of different schools out there! Don't stay and drag everyone into the same mind frame as you; the students will suffer in the long run.

- **Teaching staff:** Talk to the other teachers in your school. Have a natter over the photocopier, chat over a cup of tea, share your experiences in meetings. Keep the dialogue going amongst the professionals that you work with. Ask for help unashamedly if you are unsure of something. Support them if they ask you for help. Value and care for one another on a daily basis and you will feel and be so much stronger as a whole.

- **Front of house staff:** It might sound simple, but make sure you greet those who work at the entrance to your school and tell them how much you appreciate them once in a while! They deal with more than we know. If they were not there our jobs would be ten times harder than they are!

- **Site staff:** Make sure that you give site staff enough notice if you need help or something moving. It can be easy to moan about the shelf you have been asking them to put up for over a week now and forget just how long their to do list actually is in reality. Give them notice, give them some slack and make sure you thank them … sounds obvious but you'd be surprised!

- **Cleaning staff:** Often school cleaning staff hold more than one role in our schools and are very busy from dawn to dusk. Make sure you get to know them. A little appreciation goes a long way.

- **SLT:** The senior leadership team can get a tough old time in schools. Sometimes it is for good reason and then it is a matter for governors and official agencies to deal with. However, these cases are rare and often they get a raw deal unnecessarily. If staff become frustrated at some elements of the job they can see all the blame lying with SLT when often SLT want to change the same negative things that staff do. It is so important for staff concerns to he heard and dealt with, but we need to support our senior leaders to deal with the issues and not set them up for failure. Discuss issues openly and respectfully and offer solutions. Everyone in the school has the power to change things and we need to work together to do so.

- **Teachers from other departments:** We can become very comfortable in our own teams. Make sure you challenge yourself to get out and experience different areas of the school and share time and talk with teachers from lots of different areas. You may be surprised what you find and how inspired you can become by doing this.

- **ICT support staff:** Increasingly we are relying on ICT to deliver our lessons: interactive whiteboards, laptops, tablets, iPads and mobile devices. This is an ever-changing world and we are often working against the grain in school with old and inadequate systems due to lack of funding to support them. With this in mind, be patient with the ICT support team. They are hard workers who spend a lot of time doing things for other people every day. They are having to manage in often difficult circumstances too. Test the ICT you need well in advance, think about what could go wrong and try and pre-empt/pre-warn the ICT support team so that they can have the best opportunity to help you out.

- **Headteacher:** Boy oh boy … what a job to do. The job of a headteacher is a wonderful but highly pressurised one. The weight of the world often sits comfortably on their shoulders. It can be a lonely place up there at the top and we would do well to remember that. They have the best of times and the worst of times to deal with. Sometimes you will not know the ins and outs of certain situations because the wider staff cannot, but you need to have faith that your headteacher does what they do for the sake of the students and their well-being. We all need support, including the head.

Inspection connection

Ofsted talk about looking for an 'orderly and hardworking school community' when they visit schools. In order to be a community we need to work well in our teams. Build one another up, rejoice in our similarities and celebrate our differences. It takes time and effort to build a community in a school. A sense of community can be felt when outsiders (including Ofsted) visit, and it can make or break school.

Ofsted inspectors are guided to consider whether there is 'the highest expectations for social behaviour among the pupils and staff, so that respect and courtesy are the norm.' Students will reflect how we are with one another – they notice much more than we often realise. If we show great teamwork and respect for one another as professionals, the students will be more respectful of what we do for them. You do not have to agree with everything your teammates do and say, but respect is essential.

The following and 'consistent application' of the schools' and/or department's agreed policies is another area Ofsted will look at. Part of being a good team member is towing the line in terms of agreed policies. If you have any issues with those policies, you need to ensure you iron these out and make your peace with them in private with your line manager. You are entitled to your opinions and they should indeed be heard and considered. However you are part of a wider community and the needs of the students come first, not your own personal preferences.

Things to think about

- **In primary schools:** Take advantage of working in a small-ish team and get to know everyone in your school really well. Get out of your classroom and go and visit your colleagues. Teaching can be a very isolating experience. Visit classrooms and talk to colleagues from across the phases; Year 6 teachers and nursery teachers can all learn from each other. Our colleagues are a great resource and their rooms can be full of great ideas. Aim to have lunch or a tea break in the staffroom at least a couple of times a week, and talk to other teachers and teaching assistants. Building positive relationships across the school will make your day much happier and may even get you access to the secret Pritt stick supply.

- **In secondary schools:** The day is so busy and the school staffing system so vast that the job of getting to know people outside of your own small bubble can seem overwhelming – it is really worth it though, so make a little time and make it often.

Developing your practice

Team up with someone in your team who has a completely different skill set to you and work on a project together. Have regular reflective periods during your project and work together to go outside of your individual professional comfort zones.

Note of caution

If you do ever need to address difficult issues with a member of your team, do not avoid it, but make sure there is a neutral witness present. It is important that we are open with one another but are also mindful of other people's feelings in the process. The key to all actions in a team is mutual respect and consideration.

Online resources

- Skill set questionnaire
- Team skills reflection sheet
- Project planner
- Birthday calendar template
- Thank you postcards

8
Parents and carers

"My daughter was a golden student of the week this week!"

Year 5 parent

The area is grey; concrete jungle is too pretty a description. The tube station sits at a relentlessly busy roundabout that is approached at each side by a large road leading to various other surrounding grey areas. The imposing grey blocks of flats loom heavily as they spill into three menacing estates. On the far side of the roundabout lies a beacon of hope; a school. My school. Our outdated, crumbling buildings and extra tall metal fencing don't discourage our students from coming in too early and not leaving until we lock the gates. Our school is a haven for lots of our students who live in very challenging circumstances in terms of poverty and safety. This makes our links with families all the more important. If we didn't know our families and bring them along with us then we would have a great struggle to get on with learning in the classroom. The community events we host over the course of the academic year are vital to link us and our students' families. The times that school staff and families come together are so special.

As with your students, know your families well. It may seem like a lot of effort to get to know the families of all the students you teach, but in the long-run it will save you time, effort and energy in the classroom if teacher and family are a united team. For the united team to be formed there needs to be understanding on both sides, and a mutual respect of what is right for the child.

Putting it into practice

- **Student perspective:** Most students will talk with their parents or carers about teachers on a regular basis, and it is important that you know what they may be feeding back to home so that you can ensure it is accurate and well-informed. Get student feedback on you as a teacher, the task you do in class and the topics you study regularly, and discuss the feedback with them. Don't be fearful of their words, they will not always know what is best for their learning, and it is simply part of our job to enable them to learn what works and build trust in their teachers. Having an environment where the student voice is heard is important as it avoids a build-up of misunderstanding and allows you to have a view of the class that you would not have otherwise.

- **Drop in:** Try offering the parents and carers of your classes an informal drop-in half an hour now and then to allow them to meet you, discuss any issues their children may be experiencing at home or in your subject that may affect how they are in class, and allow you to show what your subject is about and how you approach it. It may seem like more work, but it saves time and effort in the long-run as parents feel involved and will much more readily support you if there are any issues that arise in the future.

- **Communication:** It is so important to keep the lines of communication flowing between home and school. Make sure you let parents and carers know about the wonderful things their children are doing in school. I like to do a Friday afternoon positive phone call session and pick five golden students from the week to celebrate and share their achievements with parents. It makes the start to my weekend wonderful and families happy too – everyone is a winner! On the flip side, don't let issues build up and then try and bring in parents. If things need to be addressed, you need to let home know sooner rather than later and build a joint plan for overcoming the issues. Parents and carers don't want to be kept in the dark, nor do they like an angry and frustrated phone call once things have really got bad in the classroom. Stay positive and honest with home and work as a team to overcome things a student is going through. Offering a parent and carer questionnaire can be a useful tool for improvement too; it could allow you to address misconceptions or miscommunication.

- **Community:** If your school hosts community events that celebrate local culture, get involved and enjoy building the community. In our busy global society we can so easily forget the importance of community support and collaboration. Making sure that our students feel a part of their community is a great lesson and really helps them to care about their surroundings and the people they walk among everyday. Celebrating cultural heritage is a brilliant opportunity for parents to help students understand who they are and where they come from, and this builds positive attitudes towards themselves and their community. This attitude will seep into the classroom too.

Inspection connection

Ofsted takes the views of parents and carers very seriously and because of this Parent View, the Ofsted online questionnaire, was set up to allow parents to feedback directly to Ofsted about their views on the school their child attends. Ofsted may well also choose to have informal conversations with parents in the morning or afternoon when they drop off and collect their children. Parent and carer feedback can even trigger an Ofsted inspection if they deem it is necessary. If the parent feedback that is given to Ofsted is different to what we understand their views to be, then we are doing something wrong. We need to ensure we keep in regular contact with our pupils' parents so that we act upon their concerns. That way Ofsted are not bringing us any surprises and we can show them what we are doing to address any problems.

Things to think about

- **In primary schools:** The relationship between primary teachers and their students and families can be quite intense. Remember that the families are putting a great trust in you. For some of your class you may be the adult they spend most time with and you might be the most reliable and consistent influence in their lives. Try and make it an authentic and pleasurable experience for you both. If possible, be in the playground a little before the start of school, this makes you accessible to parents and carers. Share the positive as well as the negative. Something as simple as a thumbs up to a parent at the end of the day can be a powerful thing. Although they are not always compulsory for teachers to attend, it will benefit you and your students if you go to school events and support your colleagues, PTA and families. The more you put in to your school community the more you will get back.

- **In secondary schools:** Remember that parents go from having daily contact with their child's teacher to having an opportunity once a year to have a five-minute chat – this is tough. Forming a way for them to feel more involved and connected with what is going on in the classroom is beneficial to all. Whether it is occasional newsletters home, email updates, or offering half an hour here and there, it will go a long way to building a great relationship between teacher and home.

Developing your practice

Get some tea on the go and bring out a plate of biscuits. Invite your parents in for an information afternoon and get to know them in person. What can they help you with and what can you help them with? Team effort all round.

Note of caution

When involving families of your students in school-related issues, remember that they know their children so much better than you do. Respect that knowledge and ensure that you are all working together for the child. This intention needs to be at the core of any interaction between school and home; whether it is a positive or negative situation.

Online resources

- Parent voice questionnaire
- Introduction letter/email template

9

Planning

"Failing to plan is planning to fail."

Alan Lakein

I vividly remember the first time I knew that to be a good teacher and teach effective lessons you need to be able to plan well and know yourself. I was a PGCE student teacher and I had begun to gain confidence in the classroom. I was given a lesson plan from another teacher who said, 'This lesson is always great for me, and they love it! A guaranteed great lesson. Thank me later!' They skipped off smiling with satisfaction at doing a good deed. I was really grateful for the plan and resources. I read through it the night before and went in the next day to teach it just as it was laid out in the plan. About ten minutes into the lesson it was apparent from the glazed eyes and loud yawns that I was not teaching a 'great lesson' at all. I was shocked! I looked at the plan again … yes, I was following the instructions and had stuck to the timings, but it was not working. I continued the lesson with tears welling up as I dragged them through it. At the end of the lesson I realised that that type of lesson was just not 'me'. I should have planned and tweaked it for my own style and class. Planning is the key to success for a teacher.

I really love planning lessons, schemes of work and making resources for the classroom. It is a creative process and a very satisfying one at that. In my first few years in teaching, I spent a huge amount of time researching, planning and creating resources and schemes of work for my classroom. I learnt a huge amount about my own teaching style and what makes an effective lesson. I have very fond memories of collaborating with fellow teachers to update and rework some of our shared schemes of work. The process of talking through the lessons we had both taught that term and what had worked for certain students but not others was a really useful process.

Putting it into practice

- **Endgame:** When you are planning a series of lessons, always keep the endgame in mind. Keep the assessment focus and any assessment tasks you plan to use with the class with you as you plan, and weave the skills into your lessons. Start at the finish line. Think about what you want students to achieve by the end of the series of lessons or scheme of work and plan a build-up of the skills, knowledge and challenges of each lesson.

- **Collaboration:** Get together with colleagues or as a team and plan together. Share the load as you go along and engage in healthy discussions about what works. It makes for a richer lesson and more thoughtful resources. Other teachers may approach something completely differently to you, and we can all learn a lot from one another.

- **Sharing:** Although it is important to put your own stamp on lessons for them to work for you, don't try and reinvent the wheel. There are so many great resources out there to buy or available free online, that it would be silly not to use them and adapt them to your own style. If you use resources from websites, don't forget to share some of yours too – sharing is caring. There will also be a wealth of resources that the team you work with have created – get your team sharing their goods.

- **Starters:** A starter can make or break a lesson from the outset. If you open your lesson in the right way everything flows much more easily from there. A good starter will set the tone for the lesson, spark interest and judge the starting point of students so that you know where to pitch the teaching as you progress through the lesson. Make sure you link the starter to the learning objectives, whether that be subtly or overtly, for it to be meaningful. Try a thought-provoking statement or image that outlines the key ideas to focus on in the lesson. A card sort or diamond nine activity is good for ranking ideas and seeing where students' knowledge and skills are. A puzzle of some sort works well to get them really thinking about a topic or talking with one another. Getting students excited and ready for learning through an engaging, informative and clear start is a recipe for success all round.

- **Plenaries:** Plenaries are so often overlooked as time flies by in the lesson, but they can have a significant impact on what the students will take away and remember. Plenaries should always assess the learning that has taken place, refer back to the learning objectives and be linked in some way to the starter. Try an exit quiz: to leave the room at the end of the lesson they need to provide you with an answer to a question or selection of questions that are based on the lesson content. You could complete a mini whiteboard exercise to judge learning. Get them to find another person in the room to share what they have learnt in the lesson – you could get them to then feedback what one another have said they have learnt. You could mirror the starter activity to show progress of shifts in ideas from the students.

- **Lesson objectives:** If you plan nothing else, plan the lesson objectives. Lesson objectives are the glue that holds everything together in a lesson. Plot them out over the term so that you know you are focusing on the right things and that learning is building. Make the lesson objectives clear and logically-ordered through the term, and the year, and you will reap the benefits.

- **Reflection:** Regular reflection on your own lesson will lead to better teaching and learning. Reflect honestly, reflect often, and make improvements with these thoughts.

Inspection connection

Ofsted have clearly stated that they do 'not expect teachers to prepare lesson plans for the inspection.' It is your choice what you provide to help the inspector understand your lesson. Whatever you decide to provide, make it easy to view quickly as they will want to be observing what is going on in your classroom rather than spending an age reading a life history in the lesson planning documents.

They will be considering who students are 'grouped with in lessons', so it is a good idea to make this clear on a visual, easy to read seating plan highlighting the reasoning behind grouping if possible. Have good reason behind your placement of students and make this clear.

Ofsted could well discuss with students and look for evidence in books of how 'pupils' strengths and misconceptions are identified and acted on by teachers during lessons and more widely to: plan future lessons and teaching.' Your ordering of lesson content and how your have built up the learning will be evident in the lesson, from student comments and in their work. Make sure you make it clear to students as you go to help them see the journey they are taking and how they are doing, and this will look after itself.

Things to think about

- **In primary schools:** Team up and share your skills to get your planning right. You have to teach every subject in the curriculum, there is no way you can be an expert at them all. Talk to colleagues and subject coordinators. Share lessons that went well, discuss those that didn't, ask for advice and share ideas. Share the endgame with your students. They love to know why they are learning certain skills and where it is leading to.

- **In secondary schools:** When you are planning, make sure that you are speaking to teachers in other departments so that you can see where topics may cross the curriculum. It may be that history and art are both teaching topics in the same term as English: use this to your advantage and keep the lines of communication open. Plan lessons that will enable the students to see links across the subjects – they love this.

Developing your practice

Give your students options in their learning plans. It could be that there are two schemes of work on offer for them to vote for. You could even invite parents to vote or at least discuss with their children what scheme of work would be best. If students feel involved in the planning and shaping of their own learning then they will instantly be more connected to what is going on in the classroom.

Note of caution

Be mindful not to make your planning overly fussy. If you are beginning to feel like a juggling circus clown in the classroom, the chances are you have over-planned and the lesson will be excessively teacher-led and too complex to be truly effective. As a rule of thumb: keep it simple, challenging and interesting.

Online resources

- AfL planner
- EAL planner
- Scheme of work self-reflection
- Scheme of work student questionnaire
- Scheme of work student voting form
- Starter and plenary ideas

10
Marking and feedback

"I think it's very important to have a feedback loop, where you're constantly thinking about what you've done and how you could be doing it better."

Elon Musk

In my NQT year I remember sitting down with my first ever pile of exam papers. I sat with those papers on my lap for what seemed like an eternity. I remember starting to sob as the hours slipped into the next day and the pile looked exactly the same as it had done when I started. That weekend of marking the most dull exam paper you could ever imagine nearly broke me. I then decided that I needed to get better at marking and went about doing just that. Granted, it was a slow process; but I did it!

Marking is the one thing that teachers always say is a constant uphill battle in their job. The sheer volume of marking is a leaning tower of stress in a teacher's life. The heap of books swallowing up the desk at the end of each day is a cause of dread for many of us. Nowadays, I personally love a bit of marking – I'm not saying I have always been a perfect marker and never fallen behind, but I do enjoy marking and I know there are great benefits to well thought out, targeted and reflective marking. You *have* to find a way to make it work for us and our students.

Putting it into practice

- **Marking rota:** How about trying a marking rota? I know this technique will not suit all, but for some it takes all the stress and hassle out of the marking game, so it is worth a try! Create a long list with all the classes (secondary) or subjects (primary) and list the students that you teach under each group. (For primary you will have to repeat the class list under each subject.) Then you simply need to allocate each entry on the list to groups that you will mark in a specific order on a specific set day. Add up the total entries of student names you have on your list, decide how many books you can manage to mark per day then divide the first figure by the second. The result is the number of days of your marking. For instance – a secondary teacher teaches 150 students and wants to mark 15 books every afternoon – 150/15 = 10. This means that you have a clear ten day cycle of marking: you do a little each day and your work is done. If you keep the cycle always in the same rotation then students will know exactly when their books will be marked. It could work for you – give it a try and see!

- **Leave a page:** One technique that can work well for students is to get them into the habit of expecting to leave a page after each piece of work that you are going to mark. On this page they should expect to see feedback and targets once you have marked it and a good half of the page should then be left for them to respond to your marking and make an action plan for improvement. You will have to model this process and train the students to be able to interpret your marking and break it into workable actions. It can be very powerful once students get the hang of it. You could even have a rule that the next piece of work needs to include what they have committed to improve and they should clearly mark it out so you can see their progress.

- **Verbal feedback given:** A real timesaver is a 'verbal feedback given' stamper. Keep the stamper in hand as you circulate and read students work as they write. If you see something a student could improve, give the book a stamp, tell the student what you would like them to improve on, get them to write it next to the stamper and act on it.

- **Peer and self marking:** Getting students trained up as super self and peer markers is a must. The key to this is ensuring that they always know what the success criteria is and how they can achieve it. Modelling what you want their marking to look like is also important. They can see your marking in their books as an example, but actually marking a piece of work in front of them and verbalising the thinking process that goes into what you write down is the key to their success. Then just get them into a routine and you are done.

- **Multiple choice:** Multiple choice is not used as much as it used to be and is often see as a bit of a cop-out. I beg to differ. There is some great thinking going on when teachers have really put time and effort into the multiple choice questionnaires to check knowledge and understanding. Think about whether you could bring the occasional multiple choice question into your lessons and save yourself some marking time whilst still getting a clear picture of student progress.

- **Digital marking:** If you are lucky enough to have computer access or a BYOD (Bring your own device) policy, then you could try getting students to submit work electronically and give them digital feedback. Tools like Google Drive and Edmodo lend themselves to this approach and the students really respond well to it.

- **Teaching assistants:** Don't forget to utilise your teaching assistants. Provide them with a clear and user-friendly guide to your marking style and ask them to go around and look for grammatical errors as the students work. Split the class and get them all done in one lesson from time to time. Works a treat!

Inspection connection

Ofsted are keen to look at evidence of 'pupils' academic achievement over time, taking account of both attainment and progress.' Your marking and feedback is a key area where this can be seen and evidenced to the outside eye. Therefore, however you conduct your marking just make sure it is clear and that the journey can be seen and tracked through it. This is important for the students, not just the Ofsted inspector! Other than looking at whole school data, this is the real life picture of what is going on to help students move forward in your classroom day in, day out, so show it off to it's best.

Inspectors are told to notice whether 'assessment is frequent and accurate and is used to set challenging work that builds on prior knowledge, understanding and skills', and a really easy way to do this is to evidence it in their books, folders or electronic portfolios. Now that does not mean that every page should be assessed in minute detail with the very next page showing progress, as this is just not the way learning works. Do it well when the time is right it; make it clear that this is an assessed piece of work and make time and space for students to reflect and learn from your feedback. When you are assessing their work, make it clear and show steps for improvements. Again this is important for the students, not just the Ofsted inspector!

When inspectors are looking at books (and they really love to do this!) they will look at 'whether marking, assessment and testing are carried out in line with the school's policy and whether they are used effectively to help teachers improve pupils' learning.' It is important to use marking as planning. If your marking shows a gap in knowledge or skills then your subsequent lessons should reflect this and fill in the gap. This is just good practice but make sure this is obvious to the students and in their books.

Things to think about

- **In primary schools:** If you get behind, your job can become completely unmanageable. When planning your lessons, make sure each day has only one set of books requiring a detailed mark to keep it manageable. Consider your marking when you plan your sequence of lessons. Which pieces or groups will need a detailed mark and when can students self or peer assess? What is the purpose of your marking? Marking needs to have an impact. It could be as simple as an acknowledgment or a question to move their learning forwards. Don't set yourself unrealistic amounts of marking. Just three minutes marking each students' maths and literacy book each day could take three hours. Simple things like teaching children how to check their own work with a calculator will allow them to practise their calculator skills and to take ownership of their own assessment. Just make sure you set a rule such as all their marking must be in colour pencil so it is easily distinguished from adult annotations.

- **In secondary schools:** Getting students, especially the older ones, used to the marking criteria will help ease the load if they are trained well enough to mark some pieces of work themselves. Make sure you are honest with the students about what and when you will mark as they really will hold it against you if you let them down too often, which can lead to a breakdown in relationships with a student or class.

Developing your practice

Don't presume that the students cannot access the mark schemes that you are using to mark their work. Share them with the students regularly and train them to interpret them as you do. Give them the power to improve even before you mark, and give them feedback.

Note of caution

Peer and self marking that is not well taught can be a disastrous waste of time. Make sure the students have enough training in what they are looking for and are confident with your marking before you set them off to do it themselves.

Online resources

- Marking self-assessment
- Marking symbols handout
- Marking rota template
- Peer/self marking student handout

11

Assessment

"It's what we think we know that keeps us from learning."

Claude Bernard

I have always understood that assessment is a vital part of teaching, but the manner in which I use it has changed as time has gone by. As I have grown as a teacher my assessment techniques have developed; they have become much more subtle in some ways and much more overt in others. The most important assessment to me as a young teacher was summative assessment – assessment of learning: end of unit tests, graded essays and the like. It told me how well I had taught the unit we had just covered. There is something wholly satisfying about logging the numerical results in your mark book and watching the trends! I taught towards whatever summative assessment my class had coming up or the next two-weekly marking round, gave them the tools and then watched to see if they had learnt it. However, the issue was that once the exam was taken or the two weeks had passed since I last marked their books, it was too late to go back and correct any misconceptions or boost some students without sacrificing what I was teaching next. I used formative assessment of course, but it was not my main focus. How naive of me!

You need good quality summative assessment, no doubt about it. We are in an exam-led educational system right now and the reality is that our students need to be ready for that. But the experience of 'death by exam' is a grim one indeed and not one we should be putting our students through. Times are changing, thank goodness, and regardless of the ever-present reality of exams, we teachers know the vital importance of formative assessment to help us shape our teaching and students' learning. It is important to remember that the time that lapses between one marking session and another can leave a student far behind if we have not checked their learning as we have gone along – if this happened each time we marked, imagine how confused and far behind students would become. Formative assessment is a far more powerful beast and much more important for student progression and improvement than summative assessment. If you want to boost your students' grades then excelling at formative assessment techniques and assessment for learning, rather than just assessment of learning, is a must.

I have observed many a great teacher fail to use good-quality formative assessment in their lessons, and this has impacted on what could have been great learning. To have both, you need to include formative assessment in everything you do in class. This can take many forms and can be shaped to suit your own teaching style. If your thing is a box of tricks overflowing with lollypop sticks and traffic lights then great, just use them right. If the thought of a thumbs up sends a shiver down your spine then there are many alternatives for you, so fear not. Good-quality formative assessment for learning should be: part of effective planning focusing on how students learn, central to your classroom practice, sensitive and constructive, motivational, promoting understanding of goals and criteria, helping learners know how to improve, developing capacity for self-assessment and recognising educational achievement.

Putting it into practice

- **Learning journey**: Regular assessment for learning can be easily slotted in as you go through a lesson if you have a clear learning journey planned out for your students.

- **Lesson swerves**: Although the learning journey that you have planned out for your lesson is important, it may well become apparent through your assessment for learning that you need to take a swerve from your planned route. Embrace any learning swerves that occur; it means that you are being reactive to your students' needs and not just blindly sticking to your plan for the lesson. If there is a concept that needs clarifying or an activity that needs tweaking, then do it and share the fact that you are doing this with the students to help any others that may have been struggling with the same thing.

- **Learning objectives**: I am a strong believer that if you plan nothing else formally in advance for your lessons over a term, plan all of your learning objectives. That way, you know what you want to achieve over the time frame and you can form the activities around a strong foundation that you know is culminating in an endgame that you have carefully planned for your lessons and the students' learning. Assessment for learning stops along the way should always be focused on or towards the learning objectives you have specified for the lesson, so that the students can see the point of the activity and the learning that is taking place.

- **Feedback**: Your feedback both in lessons and in books is vital to your students' learning progression. Ensure that you give dedicated time to their interaction with your marking and feedback. They need to fully understand how you mark and what you expect them to do with that marking. Always provide students with time to reflect and improve on work when you have spent precious time marking it.

- **Self and peer assessment**: Teach students how to mark their own and other's work. It can be done, it just takes time, clear explanation and practice. You can try guided marking frameworks for students to use such as 'two stars and a wish' or something similar. You could also set up a study buddy system where students always work with and assess the same peer – this can help them learn and perfect the process quicker as they can discuss the process with their buddy to improve. The key to this being useful and not just them playing teacher, is their understanding of the success criteria they are working towards in tasks.

- **Success criteria**: With all the changes we experience as teachers in terms of exam success criteria and the removal of National Curriculum levels, it is important to make sure that despite this our students remain clear about what we expect them to do in order to be successful in their learning. Provide examples of good practice in whatever task you are asking them to complete. Model the learning process to the students to show them how to tackle problems and become successful. Be clear about the key features you expect to see in their work and what the increase in skill might look like in these areas.

- **Assessing learning – questioning**: Plan in opportunities to ask a variety of questions in your lesson whenever you can. Questioning is a really powerful assessment tool – it can really help students explore their own learning and help you to shape your lesson according to the stage they are at. 'No hands up' and you selecting the student to answer is an old one but a good one, especially to assess the learning of specific groups of students. Try closed questions with students to assess specific learning you are looking for them to have picked up. Use open questions to spark discussion and encourage participation or debate, giving you an insight into their thinking on a topic. Use multiple choice questions, making the answers subtly different to assess the students' eye for detail and keep them on their toes in a subject being covered. If a student cannot answer your questions, invite them to choose a peer to help them answer. If a student does not answer the question fully, then bounce the question on to someone else to extend the initial answer. Also, flip it around – get the students to ask you questions on a specific topic you have been exploring as a class, to assess whether they are asking about surface information or if they are exploring more pertinent issues.

- **Assessing learning – graphic organisers**: Providing a point during the lesson for students to assess and show their learning, presenting it in a visual manner, can be real helpful. Students having to compile their thoughts and consider what they have learnt is a very important process. Graphic organisers such as Venn diagrams, card sorts, pyramid diagrams, mind maps, think-pair-share charts and KWL (know, what to know and have learnt) charts can be very revealing and really help you quickly assess gaps in knowledge and learning.

- **Never presume**: In your lessons, never presume that students know something, even if you know you taught it to them a few weeks back or that the topic was covered in detail during another part of the year. Always plan in assessment of their prior learning, and prompt and remind them if any vague looks come your way. It is better that you know before you embark on new content that there are areas students are having troubles with, rather than having to backtrack and waste more time later.

Inspection connection

The techniques mentioned on the previous pages are obviously things that need to be woven into your practice to be of any use, not wheeled out for observations or inspections – otherwise they will not have the impact they should have. Yes they show the observer what learning is happening really easily, but it also shows you and the students the exact same thing, and that is what is important here.

Ofsted will be checking that assessment for learning is 'frequent and accurate and is used to set challenging work that builds on prior knowledge, understanding and skills.' Building your understanding of the students' learning through assessment for learning will enable you to clearly assess these areas and ensure that your teaching is completely focused on their learning. Everyone is a winner.

Experiment with different ways of assessing for learning in your classroom and use the techniques that work for the students in your setting. Ofsted clearly state that 'Inspectors must not advocate a particular method of planning, teaching or assessment.' So, as long as what you are doing works and has impact then you are doing the right thing. Just make sure you show it off clearly for all to see!

Things to think about

- **In primary schools:** Reflect on the assessment for learning activities you have embedded in one subject and what they revealed, and consider how you can use this to push the students further in other subjects.

- **In secondary schools:** Make sure that you reflect on the assessment for learning activities you embedded in your lesson and what they revealed at the end of each lesson you had with a class. Use this knowledge along with your marking reflections to shape or reshape your medium- or long-term plan for the class.

Developing your practice

Involve your students wholly in the assessment for learning process. Talk with them about how and why you assess their learning at different points in the lesson. Get them to lead some of the activities that help you assess the other students' learning and they will see first-hand what you see and how you shape the lesson to suit their needs.

Note of caution

Assessment for learning has come under fire in the past as some teachers have fallen into the trap of rolling out an assessment for learning activity just to tick a box. Make sure whenever you are including a pause in the lesson for an assessment for learning activity, that it is specifically used to shape the remainder of the lesson or learning in the lesson or sequence of lessons.

Online resources

- Termly objective planner proforma
- Think-pair-share chart
- KWL chart
- Pyramid chart
- Venn diagram

12

Behaviour management

"When someone behaves badly in class my teacher always makes sure we stop and talk about how we should behave towards each other."

Year 5 student

I remember when it first dawned on me just how vital relationships were to becoming an effective teacher. I had been struggling with one student for a few weeks and she would just not fall into line. Every lesson was the same; disruption and defiance ruled. She would walk in, we would lock eyes and that was it, game on. 'Miss, are we doing something boring again today?' A comment that I would ignore as I directed her to her seat. 'I hate that teacher,' she would whisper to anyone who would listen. It broke my heart a little but more than that … it made me angry. How dare she criticise me, I'm a trained professional! Lesson after lesson we battled. It was draining. I remember after one particularly difficult lesson where she had compared me to her previous teacher who was apparently perfect and 'nothing like me because I was a rubbish teacher.' Standing in the middle of my empty classroom I sobbed, not just a little cry, a proper shoulder-shaking sob. One of the other teachers who worked in the room opposite me must have heard the subhuman noise coming from my classroom because she poked her head in. I sobbed at her while attempting to explain what I was upset about through my red-faced tears. She smiled knowingly at me and said something that has stayed with me ever since: 'She thinks you don't like her. Change how you approach her and find a way to connect. She is a child, you create the relationship you have with her. It is not easy to do but you have to do it.' So I did … and it worked! The worst thing you can do in your relationship with a student is to make them feel unloved.

We deal with human emotion all day long as teachers. It trudges through the gate in the morning, giggles in the group activities, slouches in the classroom chairs, skips across the playground, trails through the hallways, bounces in the canteen queue, rolls its eyes in the assembly hall and waves as it leaves to go home for the day. Schools see it all in a day – and then some more! We need to be empathetic towards our students whilst remaining detached enough to stay strong and enable them to gain the upmost that they can while they are with us. Behaviour is always linked to emotions, more so than ever with children and young people. We do not have control over the lives that our students have outside school, and we only have a certain amount of control over the behaviour system in our own schools, but we do have full control over how we approach negative and positive behaviour in our classrooms. We are the kings and queens of our lessons and we create the climate. No mean feat.

Putting it into practice

- **Outside the classroom:** Your approach to behaviour management can be reinforced by your actions outside the classroom. Take a walk at break and lunch to see your students in a non-formal setting. Get out there and join in with a football game or cheer from the sidelines if that is not your thing. Greet them as you walk around the school and bump into one another, ask them how their day has been and what they are proud of today. Find out which clubs your students enjoy taking part in and talk with them about it. Speak with their tutors and find out more about them as people, and then include some of this knowledge in a subtle way when you plan and deliver lessons. The impact of knowing your class well – both in terms of their ability in your subject, and outside the classroom – will make behaviour management ten times easier as they know you are interested and care about them.

- **Clear expectations:** Set out your expectations in no uncertain terms from the outset and stick to them. Plan them carefully before the year begins and have your behaviour rules clearly displayed in your room to refer to if students momentarily forget what is expected of them. Take the time to go through the expectations in detail, giving them the reasoning behind each rule so that they are clear. Routinely remind students about what is expected of them and do not assume that they will remember. You can offer to add expectations to the list if you wish to involve them in the creation of the classroom atmosphere. You could also provide a teacher/student contract for one and all to sign at the start of the year to ensure that they are taking the expectations seriously.

- **Make it manageable:** When you are setting up your classroom, make sure that your expectations and behavioural management systems are manageable. I have seen many a well-meaning teacher set up elaborate systems to manage positive and negative behaviours in the classroom, only to find that they simply cannot keep on top of maintaining their own system. Keep your approach to rewards and sanctions clear and simple for you and the students alike to avoid this.

- **Follow through:** If you say that you are going to issue a reward or a sanction, make sure you follow through and do it. You are breaking the student's trust if you don't. If you say you will be making a positive call home then do it or you will find students are less bothered about behaving well for you as you have shown that you do not care. If you say you will be holding a student back for ten minutes at the end of the lesson, ensure you follow through and do just that or you will be sending a clear message to the rest of the class that you will not deal with bad behaviour. Do what you say you are going to do.

- **Keep calm:** Teachers really must stay connected to their inner calm. If you lose your calm approach then you have lost control of the situation. It is so easy to get swept up in the emotions that some young people vent in school. If we mirror their anger and frustration or react in an emotional way, the situation will very likely escalate to an unmanageable level. We must be the calm in the storm or expect to feel the full force of the winds. You don't need to turn off your emotions in order to do this, just keep them in check so you can clearly deal with the situation.

- **Don't take it personally:** Growing up is tough. There will be times when students say something that hurts, whether it is intentional or not. Students are curious about their teachers and spend a large amount of their day looking at them. From time to time they may blurt out an observation about you that is not particularly welcome. Forgive them and talk with them about it openly. We do need to be self-aware; if we have ears that stick out, untameable hair that grows in an unusual way or wonderfully large feet, then expect students to mention this at some point. It is natural; it is not personal. Students will also say things in anger, frustration, or in the heat of the moment. If this happens, don't avoid appropriate sanctions; address it, put an appropriate sanction in place and move on together.

Inspection connection

The Ofsted outstanding criteria for behaviour talks about the students having a 'thirst for knowledge and understanding and a love of learning,' and the clear impact that this has on their progress in lessons. Behaviour is not just about following school rules and answering back, it really is about students having a positive attitude to their own learning and progression in school. Some students will have this already and others will need help – that is where you come in. Ensuring that you model and encourage this behaviour is so important.

Inspectors will be looking for evidence of pupils being 'keenly aware of how good attitudes and behaviour contribute to school life, adult life and work.' When we are setting up expectations, rewarding positive behaviour or correcting negative behaviour, it is important to ensure we talk about the why. Why is it important to act in a certain manner in certain situations? How will it benefit them in their school life and beyond to follow the guidelines set out for them in your school community? Don't presume students automatically know this or that they don't need reminding regularly.

Things to think about

- **In primary schools:** When you see a student's parents at the start or end of the day, take the opportunity to share any positive praise as well as voicing any concerns about behaviour early on so they can fully support you in dealing with the situation.

- **In secondary schools:** The logistics of the school day make sanctions a little more complex for secondary teachers. If you have issued a short detention but your lesson does not fall before break, lunch or the end of the day, you will not be able to keep that student behind. You must still follow up as soon as possible, or the student will have no memory of the misdemeanour. Send a note with a reliable student to the next teacher asking them to hold onto the student in question. Ensure your next class leave on the bell and quickly make your way over to the classroom the student is in. It gets the sanction out of the way and shows a united front as teachers are working together.

Developing your practice

Remain calm and consistent in your approach to behaviour management and you will stay clearly focused on positive behaviour. Celebrate that loudly and clearly.

Note of caution

Whatever your personal beliefs in terms of behaviour management, make sure you are working within the bounds of the school rules and guidelines. If you are a lone wolf who manages the behaviour in their own classroom well but are in stark opposition to the school system, then you will be confusing the students in the long-run. If they do not have a consistent approach from all teachers it becomes a 'divorced and arguing parents' situation: not pretty for anyone involved and the students will be the ones to suffer.

Online resources

- Classroom expectations poster
- Student teacher contract

13

Literacy and numeracy

"If you don't get the basics right then the rest of the work you do will never be as good on paper as it was in your head."

Year 8 student

Regardless of the age, stage or subject that you teach, the key skills that students need to be successful in when they leave the cocoon of the classroom are wide and varied, at the core of which sit the essentials that are literacy and numeracy. Without these two key skills, making sense of the world is an epic task. It is very important to remember that we are all teachers of literacy and numeracy.

A literate student is one who is confident with reading, writing, speaking and listening in any context and able to use this to navigate adult life. Literacy, however, is much more than just the mechanics of these individual skills. It is the connections between each skill, across subject areas. It involves thought, understanding, exploration, recall, selection and analysis. It incorporates coherent, considered and convincing communication in talking and writing. That is no mean feat and needs us all on board for students to achieve this to a proficient level.

A student leaving school numerate means that they are able to cope confidently with the mathematical needs of adult life. Skills that we can all help with, regardless of the subject being taught, include accuracy of measurement, calculation, estimation, data handling, graphical work, use of graphs and diagrams, reasoning and problem solving. Ensuring that key mathematical vocabulary is being used across the curriculum, and unambiguously, is essential for the embedding of mathematical skills they need in life without confusion.

Putting it into practice

- **Literacy – writing:** When you are setting writing tasks in the subject you are teaching, make sure you share examples of excellent writing in the style you are wanting them to write in, and share the key features of the type of writing you are asking them to produce. Model on the board how you might want them to plan, think and do their writing. Regular exploration and reminders about the use of punctuation is essential for all ages. Discuss punctuation with your students and ask them to make sure they include certain punctuation in their writing in different lessons. Simple displays around your classroom to remind students of the rules are always helpful.

- **Numeracy – symmetry:** If you use visuals in your lesson, can you discuss the symmetry of the image you are using?

- **Literacy – vocabulary:** Ensure you discuss key subject-specific vocabulary with students, including the different ways these words may be used in different contexts to avoid confusion. Explore synonyms for words that are used often so that they can easily vary their vocabulary. Having displays or handouts of key vocabulary is a great tool for the classroom.

- **Numeracy – interpreting and discussing results:** An important branch of mathematics is statistics, which involves the collection, presentation and evaluation of data. If you are collecting information in your subject for a presentation or piece of work, can you make the mathematical links to show the transferrable skill?

- **Literacy – spelling:** Identify commonly misspelt words and explore with the students strategies for learning and remembering those words, such as phonetics, grammatical rules, visualisation, root words and their meanings or mnemonics.

- **Numeracy – proportion:** Can you highlight and examine the use of proportion in recipes, experiments or words, for example, to achieve different outcomes?

- **Literacy – reading:** Make sure that you incorporate frequent opportunities for students to read aloud to the class or smaller groups. Don't be put off by time constraints or lack of student skills – how else will they improve? When reading texts together, make sure you stop and discuss both obvious and more subtle meanings with the students. Explore the vocabulary that you come across with your students and how the words are used.

- **Numeracy – grid references:** Could you use grid references or coordinates in your lesson in some way – locating an item on a map or an image?

- **Literacy – textual organisation:** Highlight the organisation of any texts you read or create in class. Discuss the different options the students have in terms of ordering their written work, and what impact they have upon the reader.

- **Numeracy – representing data:** There are many reasons you may collect data of one kind or another in class. Can you incorporate the use of charts or graphs to represent the findings of something you have been investigating or studying in your lesson?

- **Literacy – speaking:** Providing opportunities for students to build their confidence in formal academic-focused speaking is essential in all subjects. Making sure that students are speaking in the way you would like them to write is half the battle. If they can say it, they can write it. The more you do this with students, the better they become and the more useful it is for the learning process.

- **Numeracy – timelines and sequencing:** Can you find opportunities to place events in chronological order in different subjects, for example historical events, the plot of a story or the paragraphs of a piece of reading?

- **Literacy – note-making:** Explore with your students the skills needed to be excellent note makers in different subjects. Don't presume they will be able to do this, break it down. Model and scaffold the process involved such as not writing every word, how to decide what is important, active listening, how to abbreviate, using colour or highlighters, being consistent, improving handwriting and paraphrasing.

- **Numeracy – time, distance and speed:** Using music or moving image in your lesson gives you a great opportunity to discuss and analyse the use of time, distance and speed. For instance thinking about the difference in speed of different camera shots, or the varying distances of different camera angles.

- **Literacy – active listening:** When there is a text being read aloud or a student giving an extended answer or presentation to the class, it is a great idea to train the students to be active listeners. Ask them to formulate questions about what they have listened to, highlight the best vocabulary they heard or summarise the main points. Keep them on their toes and make sure they are trying to process what they are listening to all the time.

- **Numeracy – substituting into formulae:** There are a number of subjects where the practice of substituting into formulae (where different variables are represented by letters) is relevant in order to explore different input and output.

Inspection connection

The importance of numeracy and literacy across all subjects is now very clearly woven into the core of the Ofsted school inspection handbook. Regardless of whether students are five or 15, the importance of these skills never wanes. They are so vital to success in life after school in every part of the working world that we cannot avoid their importance in our key stage or subject area.

In the Ofsted outstanding criteria for the general quality of education in a school they state that they will be looking for 'excellent practice that ensures that all pupils have high levels of literacy and mathematical knowledge, understanding and skills appropriate to their age.' Knowing what is expected of them in terms of literacy and numeracy at any particular age is our duty.

When Ofsted are looking at outstanding teaching in a school they will be expecting to see that 'the teaching of reading, writing, communication and mathematics is highly effective and cohesively planned and implemented across the curriculum.' This clearly mentions the need for these skills to be woven into the fabric of every subject being taught.

For Ofsted, outstanding achievement in a school would include students being able to 'acquire knowledge and develop and apply a wide range of skills to great effect in reading, writing, communication and mathematics.' They go on to mention the necessity of this for students' next stage in education, training or employment. These are lifelong skills that we must not assume students are secure in.

Things to think about

- **In primary schools:** Having the students with you for most of the time is a great opportunity to very quickly embed and practise the cross-curricular nature of numeracy and literacy. Ensuring that the skills they need are interwoven throughout the day will lead to them very quickly becoming second nature.
- **In secondary schools:** Ensuring that your students see the relevance of literacy and numeracy in your subject and how that impacts on life outside of the classroom and after school, is a great way for students to really buy into putting their efforts into becoming better with literacy and numeracy all of the time.

Developing your practice

Design and display some literacy and numeracy posters showing the skills you want your students to be using all of the time, and reminding them of how they can best demonstrate them in their approach to speaking, reading, listening and writing. Even better, get the student to design them!

Note of caution

Don't see literacy and numeracy as something to tag on to your lesson but as an essential part of all subjects that needs to become second nature to the students. If you are not confident about your own skills then do a bit of research and make sure you brush up on the basics.

Online resources

- Spelling strategies poster

14

Spiritual, moral, social and cultural education

"To educate a man in mind and not in morals is to educate a menace to society."
Theodore Roosevelt

I have always enjoyed discussing life, morality, culture, society and spirituality with my students, right from the start. I started my teaching career in an inner London school in a deprived area and have remained in London ever since. I personally enjoy working in an inner-city environment where they is a real mix of cultures and life experiences. I loved that the students' lives were so different; it allowed us to discuss and debate differences from a first-hand perspective rather than in theory. Weaving spiritual, moral, social and cultural (SMSC) elements into my lesson was natural for me and I loved the connection it gave the students with the lesson content. They felt it was relevant to them personally or their peers straight from the outset.

That is not to say that including SMSC education in a non-urban school setting cannot be just as satisfying in a different way. It can be! Educating the whole child is so important and relevant to every student we teach in every lesson. Life lessons are just as important as the subject-specific content we deliver to our students. We should be finding a way to marry the two together and providing our students with a rounded academic, spiritual, moral, social and cultural education all of the time.

The four key elements of SMSC education are directly covered in PSHE and citizenship lessons in all schools, but teachers of all subject areas and year groups should be including these elements in their lessons. All four elements are of equal importance in all the guidance provided so should be covered equally where logical. Spiritual development refers to the exploration and reflection of beliefs, religious or otherwise, and respect of others' beliefs in the world around them. Moral development refers to the students' ability to recognise and debate moral and ethical rights and wrongs in their own and others' lives and how that is covered by the law. Social education refers to the students' ability to investigate moral issues, appreciate a range of topics, participate and cooperate with others in a group setting, resolve conflicts effectively, engage with the fundamental values of British democracy and contribute positively to their community. Cultural development refers to the students' ability to understand their own and others' cultures and their diversities, tolerance of differences in culture, the influence a wide range of cultures have had on shaping their own heritage and about Britain's democratic parliamentary system.

Putting it into practice

- **Spiritual:** Debate with students about the significance of different religious values. Enable students to understand how language is used in different ways to communicate. Explore images, music and language and how they can inspire feelings of awe and wonder. Help students explore controversial issues in history. Explore with students the feelings and values behind characters in texts you read, and talk about the different opinions between science and religion. Consider how religion influences art, literature and popular culture. You could organise a trip to a gallery, religious building or science museum to explore issues around spirituality.

- **Moral:** Help students develop and explore their understanding of what is right and wrong in real-life situations in texts and fictional situations being studied. Helping students to understand that there are different codes of conduct and etiquette in different cultures, countries, business and sports is really important, as is helping students develop a respect for others' beliefs even if they are different to their own. This can be done through debate in the classroom. Get students to consider the actions and consequences when looking at historical figures, characters in texts and real life.

- **Social:** Explore language as an aspect of social identity with the students. Discuss the impact that science, art, literature, music and religion has had upon society and their surroundings now and in the past. Include group and team activities in your lesson to hone the student's social skills. Explore the technological advances and how they have changed our lives. You could organise a trip to a museum to explore changes in society.

- **Cultural:** Explore the music, art, literature, sport, history and religion of different cultures. Foster an appreciation of different cultures and traditions in your subject. Explore how language influences and shapes cultures in different ways. Study the natural world with students and different cultural beliefs and traditions around it. Discuss with students the development of spoken and written language over time and cultural attitudes to that language. You could invite culture leaders in from the local area to share experiences with students.

Inspection connection

Under the inspection guidance sections of the Ofsted school inspection handbook there is mention of SMSC education throughout, from behaviour to leadership, early years to the provision of education. This is a key feature of good and outstanding schools when you look at inspection reports. They are looking for it to appear in lessons, assemblies, and display and be the bedrock of students attitudes of life and learning. Ofsted inspectors are guided to ensure that, before making any final judgements on a school, they must consider the effectiveness and impact of 'the provision for pupils' spiritual, moral, social and cultural development.'

The Ofsted outstanding criteria for outstanding quality of education clearly focuses on the school's provision and promotion of SMSC education across the board. They will be assessing whether 'the school's thoughtful and wide-ranging promotion of pupils' spiritual, moral, social and cultural development and their physical well-being enables them to thrive in a supportive, highly cohesive learning community.' This clearly indicates that they expect to see this across the school and not in isolated special lessons or sessions. We all have a responsibility to ensure we are doing our part to develop the whole child in our lessons.

Things to think about

- **In primary schools:** Younger children will not necessarily have a wide knowledge in spiritual, moral, social and cultural education areas, so there is a lot they can learn from your inclusion of these issues in your lesson planning. Provide opportunities for them to empathise with new and unknown situations that may arise.

- **In secondary schools:** Make sure you take advantage of the forthrightness of our teenage and nearly teenage students. The students you teach have strong opinions and they are a great resource to use to really get your teeth into spiritual, moral, social and cultural education topics in your subject area. Challenge them and open their eyes to the fascinating issues this area of teaching can raise.

Developing your practice

Consider involving parents and figures from the local community in SMSC education activities. If you have resources right on your doorstep then open up the learning to real people and real places in your community that can help the student develop their spiritual, moral, social and cultural skills and understanding.

Note of caution

When discussing or exploring SMSC education issues there may well be a clash or differences of ideas or beliefs between students. Embrace this; shape the discussion and use it as an opportunity to explore how to be tolerant of others whilst not necessarily agreeing with them. A great life lesson.

Online resources

- SMSC education Ofsted definition poster

15
Homework

"Homework can be really good...or really boring and pointless."

Year 6 student

I have loved and hated homework in equal measure at different points in my teaching career. I have looked on in despair as my top set students pile up their lovingly slaved-over masterpieces when I am already swamped with marking. But I have also felt real joy and pride in my class when they come into the lesson buzzing because they have found the answer to the question I challenged them to investigate. Now I think I have found a happy medium. I appreciate that students having work to focus on at home can create a good work ethic and, if the work is well thought out, it can broaden horizons and open up new doors of learning for students.

The key to getting homework right with your students is to make it interesting, relevant and manageable. Homework is too often overly complex, long or mind-numbingly dull, meaning students don't engage with it as they should and either give up or produce shoddy work. At the other end of the spectrum are teachers who avoid setting homework because they simply cannot bare the thought of adding to their workload and piling on more marking – or worse still, setting homework but never marking it or giving it back to the students. These are all avoidable. Homework can be manageable and useful for all involved – I promise! Ofsted will be looking for appropriate setting of homework and the impact that it has when they visit, so however you choose to set homework make sure it is enabling students to progress in their learning. They may look for evidence of homework in a number of ways, including looking at student books, checking homework records or school policies and timetables. They could also ask students and parents and carers about homework too, so ensure that you make your homework plan clear to all and stick to it.

Putting it into practice

- **Make it manageable**: Set tasks that you know you can manage to check or mark in some way fairly promptly. Or, a homework project that builds over the weeks of a term culminating in students handing in one piece of work that they have produced at the end of the period. You could consider setting homework tasks less often but placing more importance upon them by making them formally-assessed work. Have a clear plan for setting your homework. You may find, as I do, that digital submission of homework saves time as you don't need to lug books and papers back and forward, and they remain organised and filed for you if you use a tool such as Show My Homework, Google's Classroom or Edmodo.

- **Spark their curiosity**: Setting a task that will lead your students in an unexpected direction, or based on a topic that you know will really spark their interest, will increase the likelihood that they will do it, and do it well. Build up a little mystery around the homework task, don't give it all away! Set them a quiz to find the answers too. Give them clues or riddles, treasure hunt style, that they need to work out or find the answer to on the topic you are studying. A QR code treasure hunt is a fun way of doing this and only requires a smartphone to help. Provide them with a provocative statement, without explanation, on a new area of the topic you are studying and ask them to write a response.

- **Students leading the learning**: Get students to step up and lead the learning when it comes to their homework. Give them a number of options to complete over the course of a topic and allow them to choose what they do and when. It keeps them interested as they have had a say in what they do. It also caters for different tastes in the class if the task options are varied. You could even get the students themselves to decide on the homework for the class to choose from on a set topic and really hand the homework over to them. In primary, you can give the students options in their homework. Let them choose how to present their homework: a poster, leaflet, bullet points, film, PowerPoint, photographs, drawings – there are many options. Share some ideas with them and they will inspire each other.

- **Challenges:** Getting an element of competition into the homework works wonders for student motivation. Competition could be with themselves in terms of improving their score each time when being tested on a skill. Try having specific skills or knowledge that you will be looking for in their homework that will receive points or prizes if you spot them using it well. You could have a homework star of the week that students work towards for each class or subject and visually display their name to celebrate, maybe a certificate or postcard home too. You could start a league table that places different students against one another each week – draw names at the start of a half-term and set up the scoreboard for all to see in advance – similar to the World Cup. This allows students to work towards being a class winner but also allows students that may not have a chance of winning over all to win each time they do homework. This is great fun and gets them wanting to complete that work.

- **Flipped learning:** Flipping learning can take many forms. The key idea is that it gets the students taking responsibility for their own learning through connecting with core content of the skill or knowledge they need for the next lesson at home, then the time in class is spent with the students trialling out the new skill with the teacher's assistance and guidance. This can involve getting students to complete tasks, watch videos or complete reading that leads directly into the next lesson's tasks. It can also mean literally flipping the learning on its head; providing the direct instruction that traditionally takes up a significant part of the start of the lesson, perhaps in the form of videos or reading, as a homework task, so that the main activity is where you actually begin the lesson following the homework. It takes a little bit of training with students but can have real impact on how your work with the students and how they view homework.

- **Self marking:** Create opportunities for homework that can easily be self-marked or peer-marked by students during the lesson that the work is due in. Quizzes to test knowledge or skills practised for the homework is a really easy way to check their homework and see where they are so you can adapt the lesson accordingly. Also, it means a lot less marking for you and is still very useful for all students doing the homework. Try regular spelling tests on key words for each topic – no marking from you required and students are working on their literacy and vocabulary all at the same time. You could also try a comprehension quiz on a reading homework you have set them to test their understanding of the text. Using tools like Edmodo quizzes or polls or the Socrative App (there are loads more out there these are just ones I have used) allows you to test the students as soon as they enter the classroom, as well as showing trends in understanding and misunderstanding of the homework that has been set. These tools also record the results so that you can add them to your ongoing mark book for your class, which is ideal.

Inspection connection

The Ofsted outstanding criteria for teaching talks about observations being made of 'appropriate homework that, together with clearly directed and timely support and intervention, match pupils' needs accurately.' What makes any one piece of homework 'appropriate' will differ hugely depending on the age, ability and individual needs of the students that you teach. The key thing is ensuring that it is supporting learning and progression rather than filling in time at home.

Homework is one way that you can address the need to ensure that the 'most able are stretched and the least able are supported sufficiently to reach their full potential', something Ofsted says should be at the core of what we do. Clear differentiation should be evident in your setting of homework as well as in your lessons.

Things to think about

- **In primary schools:** Get parents and carers fully engaged in the homework process. If at all possible try to create homeworks well in advance and share them with your student's families so they can plan their time to help their child. Make the homework something that can really bring the child and parent together in the learning process and enjoy it together. Be mindful of the resources available to families. Not all students will have access to computers. Make sure homework is accessible to all your students. Have a place in your classroom to celebrate homework. A weekly homework wall will encourage students to take pride in their work. Acknowledge homework, give students time to share it with their peers. It does not always have to be written work – making, observing and experimenting can really inspire children. Philosophy questions are a great way to get the whole family involved. Have set days for homework to be given out and expected to be returned.

- **In secondary schools:** It is really important to make sure that there is enough time given to complete the work for the students in secondary school. Often students complain about getting lots of homework all at once or of having too tight a deadline to manage their workload well at home. Giving a good amount of time between the date set and the date due should alleviate any traffic jams in the secondary homework load. Regular discussions about how to manage independent work time at home is important for lots of secondary students too, so don't forget to give your words of wisdom on this matter.

Developing your practice

Try designing your homeworks to tier up in terms of skill and/or knowledge over a term to keep the students on their toes and allow them to make progress at home as well as in school. You could also run competitions to allow students to design homework for the class to complete based on the topic you are covering.

Note of caution

If you don't have time to mark it then don't set it. If it is a task for task's sake and you are setting it just because you feel you should set something, rather than because it will benefit your students' learning, don't set it. If you do this you will devalue homework and the students will start to not bother with it in your lessons.

Online resources

- Student homework advice poster
- World Cup style homework score chart example
- Parent advice for helping with homework handout

16

Closing the achievement gap

"There have been a few special teachers who have really helped me become a better student. I am looking forward to my future because of their help and encouragement."

Year 12 student

There are so many students who have made me realise just how important it was to make sure I do everything within my power as a teacher to give each of them the best chance of achieving, regardless of their background. Liz – who never handed in her homework and later revealed to me that it was because she shared her room with three other siblings and had nowhere to work quietly at home. Bob – who never had the right equipment or uniform when he was in school because he was always being shunted about between various family members' homes and had nowhere to keep his things that was his own. Jan – who would remind me every lesson that school was a waste of time and she didn't need any qualifications because she was going to go on benefits as soon as she could because that is what everyone in her family did. Dom – who was a persistent absentee due to the fact that he was so exhausted every day after caring for his disabled mother alone each night. These examples are just a drop in the ocean; there have been many over the years.

These students and their families need our support more than we even realise. There is no denying the fact that there exists a significant gap between students who come from disadvantaged backgrounds and those that do not. This gap exists not only across schools but also within schools up and down the country. This is a sad fact that we must not just sit back and accept as part of life. We have the power to change the opportunities that are available to our most disadvantaged pupils and really make a difference to their futures. We must take up that challenge.

Putting it into practice

- **High expectations:** Building confidence in our students is vital, and a consistent mantra of high expectations for all goes a long way to building self-belief. If students feel you have faith in them to reach the top they will step up. When planning your approaches and interventions to enable your disadvantaged pupils to progress, make sure that you always make them high in challenge and strong on support. Discussing future plans and emphasising that anything they want is within their reach with hard work is a powerful message and one that needs repeating often.

- **Parental involvement:** Reach out to the parents and carers of your disadvantaged students. Interventions that involve the whole family in their child's learning have been recorded to be the most effective. Speak with them on the phone about how their child is doing and what is going well. Help parents and carers build a learning relationship with their child with your support. Invite them in informally for an after-school session exploring simple ways that they can help their child in the learning process and support their progression from home.

- **Relationships and social and emotional learning:** Some of our students from homes that are considered to be disadvantaged may well have experienced less attention to social and emotional development and we need to fill the gap where this is the case. Building relationships with all of our students is part of the job, but where social and emotional development is lacking at home it is all the more important that we help students learn these life lessons along with us in the classroom. Explore rights and wrongs openly, encourage empathy and discuss emotions that are involved in human relationships and how to cope with these.

- **Equipment:** Ensure that you have sufficient equipment available in the classroom for those times when a student genuinely does not have the right equipment through no fault of their own but a lack of funds or their personal circumstance. The last thing you want to do is cause a scene about equipment if the reasons behind the lack of it is a sensitive one – it can be damaging to the relationship with that student.

- **One-to-one or small group teaching:** You could consider organising one-to-one or small group sessions for a selection of pupils, including any of those from a disadvantaged background that need support. The power of a more intensive approach to gaps in learning is huge, not just in terms of academic advancement but in the building of the students' confidence when back in class. If you can run a lunchtime session great, if not then make sure that the staff member is able to deliver the content sufficiently for the session to be effective.

- **Modelling and scaffolding:** Some students from disadvantaged homes may not have access to a wide range of reading materials and resources to pull their ideas from. Providing good quality reading material and examples for students to study in class can bridge the gap. Ensuring that you talk through choices writers make and unfamiliar situations and vocabulary that may crop up will also help in this area. Help students see how they can translate excellent models you provide into their own work.

- **Peer interaction and mutual support:** Buddying students up from different backgrounds can be a great way of allowing pupils to see different perspectives and guide one another to be better. Allowing students to work together independently is a skill that needs to be taught well. It is important that students learn the etiquette of professional working relationships outside of just working with their friendship group. It is particularly important to encourage lower-achieving pupils, whether they are from disadvantaged backgrounds or not, to talk about and articulate their learning when working together with others to ensure that they do not contribute less.

- **Feedback and monitoring – target setting, AfL, use of data:** Providing effective feedback is challenging. Research suggests that it should be specific, accurate and clear (for example, 'It was good because you …' rather than just 'correct'). Compare what a learner is doing right now with what they have done wrong before (for example, 'I can see you were focused on improving X as it is much better than last time's Y ...'). Encourage and support further effort although make sure it is given sparingly so that it is meaningful; provide specific guidance on how to improve rather than just telling students when they are wrong. Find further support through effective professional development for teachers.

Inspection connection

The Ofsted outstanding criteria for achievement of pupils clearly states that attainment and progress of disadvantaged pupils must 'at least match or are rapidly approaching those of other pupils nationally and in the school.' They do recognise and mention that there are barriers to learning for our disadvantaged pupils, but their stance is a clear and well-intentioned one – we must overcome these barriers.

Ofsted also say that in order for teaching to be judged as outstanding, all pupils including those who are disadvantaged should be 'making sustained progress that leads to outstanding achievement.' It is no longer about seeing those one-off outstanding lessons where the teacher is a star and the pupils are performing well in the flesh. The outstanding teaching is judged over time and with a focus on real and actual progress.

Ofsted will gather their view of how disadvantaged pupils are doing in the school through looking at the school data initially, but also through observing them in and around the school site; in the classroom as well as 'informally before and after school, at lunchtime and during break or play times. During informal conversations with pupils, inspectors must ask them about their experiences of learning and behaviour in the school.' This is another reason to ensure that students are fully involved in their learning and the processes and reasoning behind what you guide them through in lessons – so that they know why they are doing what they are doing.

Things to think about

- **In primary schools:** Ensure that you are really connecting with the families of your disadvantaged children. There will be many different reasons behind a student's family being classified as disadvantaged and the more you know the better you can support them. Work with the parents or carers to raise their aspirations where necessary.

- **In secondary schools:** Ensure that you are exploring what students can do with your subject once they leave school. Encourage them to think widely about their life choices and ensure they understand that they have the same options as everyone else they just need to choose them and work hard towards them.

Developing your practice

Use the learning environment to encourage the behaviours you want to see in your students. Get some aspirational posters up around your classroom that encourage the behaviours and thought processes that you want to see in all of your students, regardless of their background.

Note of caution

Although it is very important for teachers to ensure that we are doing all we can to remove the barriers that our disadvantaged students face, we must be careful not to make them feel as if they are different in a negative way. We do not want to single anyone out and make them feel uncomfortable. Handle your chosen approach with sensitivity and care.

Online resources

- Aspirations poster

17

Special educational needs

"Every child deserves a champion; an adult who will never give up on them, who understands the power of connection and insists that they become the best that they can possibly be."

Rita Pierson

Having a special educational need should not hold any student back. We have a duty to ensure we do all we can to give every child the same opportunities regardless of their learning needs. There is a huge amount information out there to help teachers work more effectively with those students in their class who have specific and perhaps more demanding needs than others in the class – you must use that knowledge to inform your teaching. Use your school SENCO to help and advise you, and enjoy the variety that all your students bring to the classroom environment.

Putting it into practice

- **Inclusion:** If your students with special educational needs (SEN) are not making progress, then inclusion is not going to be graded as good or better in an inspection. All students should be progressing and you should be intervening in whatever way you see appropriate to enable them to if they are not. Differentiation by task, support or outcome should be carefully thought out and planned into the lessons and schemes of work with your specific class in mind. Everyone deserves to achieve their very best and our job is to create the environment to enable them to do this.

- **Data**: Knowing your students' data is essential for planning your lessons and for interventions. Knowing them as people is an obvious essential but it must be alongside the data you have on them in terms of prior assessment data and strengths and weaknesses. The very best way we can help our students with SEN is by making them feel valued as a person and pushing them as academics just as we would any other student in our class – with appropriate support in place to aid them.

- **Paperwork**: Making sure you have your paperwork in order and easily accessible is an easy win in terms of showing an external assessor or visitor to your class the overview of the students, including the students with SEN. Have a folder ready to be viewed in your class that has been updated after each reporting cycle or assessment, and has essential, easy to view documents outlining the overview of your class. Have a class profile that has listed in it all students in the class, prior assessment data such as SATs or KS2/3/4 data, EAL status, SEN status, first language, whether they are looked after, whether they are gifted and talented and anything else you feel is relevant. Have a clear seating plan with data and student info mapped out on the plan. These documents, once created, do not take much time to alter when new data is available from tests or a different focus is needed. They really do make it much easier for the visitor or assessor to get to know your class, but more importantly the process of completing these documents helps you become more familiar with your class and makes you think about where you are seating them and what support you are offering them.

- **Interventions**: If any students, including your students with SEN, are not progressing as they should then appropriate interventions need to be looked at sooner rather than later to get them up to speed and back on track. Intervention could, among other things, involve a teaching assistant working with a student inside or outside of the classroom or specific grouping to aid progression. Whatever the interventions are that you have chosen to put in place for your students who are not progressing, it is a necessity to check their impact – if they are having none then you need to change them and try something new with that student. Make sure you have a summary or clear reference to any interventions noted briefly on the class profile for ease of reference.

- **Teaching assistant in secondary schools**: Secondary teachers, if you are lucky enough to have a teaching assistant in your classroom make sure you plan for how to use them. Try and speak to them in advance and provide them with any essential resources that may help them. Get them focusing on specific students and making sure they are keeping up with the learning. Sit them with a specific group and set that group a special task linked to the lesson content that the teaching assistant helps them with and which they present back to the class at the end of the lesson; it makes working with the teaching assistant an exciting prospect. Get the teaching assistant marking for general grammatical errors in the students' books as they work – this helps with your marking and also makes the students value the teaching assistant's opinion on learning and lesson content as they are seen as important. Get the teaching assistant leading starters or plenaries with your or the students' help from time to time. However you use them, make sure you do, as they can be a really beneficial aid to every student in your class.

- **Teaching assistant in primary schools**: The role of the teaching assistant in primary schools has changed dramatically over recent years. Get to know your teaching assistants, find out their strengths and what they need from you in order to make the biggest impact on learning. Plan with your adult support in mind and make sure you and your TA spend time supporting students with SEN. Get them to start and supervise an activity but make sure students with SEN still have time to practise working independently. In an ideal world, teaching assistants would have time with teachers before and after lessons to go through plans and feedback, but often they have other responsibilities in the school and this is not possible. Find simple ways to communicate, such as brief Post-its to keep you connected. Set achievable regular targets for students with SEN and share them with TAs. This will allow them to use their initiative with resources and activities.

Inspection connection

Ofsted are looking for evidence of an 'inclusive environment that meets the needs of all pupils' and it is our duty to do our bit in our classrooms to ensure that that is the case. A pupil having a special educational need should not be a reason for them not to progress. It should be a matter that we address every day in our classrooms to ensure that they have what they need to give them an equal opportunity.

The Ofsted outstanding criteria for achievement of pupils highlights the fact that they will be looking at the data attached to special educational needs students in the school and expecting to see that learning 'is consistently good or better.' Make sure you know the needs of all of your students and are well informed as to what works with your special educational needs students.

Often Ofsted will take a 'small sample of case studies in order to evaluate the experience of particular individuals and groups, such as … those who have special educational needs.' This means that they may well focus specifically on what we are doing for those pupils to ensure they are getting the best possible chance in school. If you have a teaching assistant working with special educational needs students in your class, then they will be looking at how you work with that teaching assistant to get the most out of them in the classroom for that student. Make sure you highlight what you do in your classroom to the inspection team to make this a reality for your students with special educational needs.

Things to think about

- **In primary schools:** If you have a teaching assistant that is attached to your class then bring them into your planning sessions, or part of them. Ensure they know well in advance your schemes of work and get them working intensely with students who are in need and/or not progressing as they should. Students with SEN can really be challenged and supported to achieve their best with two of you working as a team. Work together and well and you have a dream team right there that your secondary counterparts would be envious of.

- **In secondary schools:** You deal with a huge number of students so it is really important that you know who your students with SEN are, what there needs are and approaches you can take with them. Discuss your students with SEN with the SENCO, look at the guidance that your school provides of different special education needs and follow the strategies they suggest for specific needs. Planning for your students with SEN is a must or they will drift in the sea of secondary school and slowly sink.

Developing your practice

Make sure you speak regularly with the parents or carers (or if your school prefers – the tutor) of your students with SEN so that you are aware of the whole child. When things are tough, as they often are for teenagers, our students with SEN can feel it worse than most. Be prepared and considerate in these times of challenge.

Note of caution

Students with SEN can pose a challenge in our classrooms, and it is a challenge that we must rise to in order to ensure that the next generation is the best there has been, regardless of previous or present special needs. We have a duty to do all that we can to get the very best out of our students with SEN. Never make excuses for a student with SEN not achieving – look for a way to help them start achieving. High expectations should be for all.

Online resources

- Class profile proforma
- Ways to use your teaching assistant handout

18

Appraisal and performance management

"We are told that talent creates its own opportunities. But it sometimes seems that intense desire creates not only its own opportunities, but its own talents."

Eric Hoffer

I think I am quite good at being managed. I have always enjoyed meeting with my line managers and planning for my progression. I will always voice my opinions professionally but also tow the line and represent the school well. I will never put down my line managers; I respect them even if I don't agree with everything they say. I have genuinely wanted to learn from each and every line manager I have had. I also enjoy when they challenge and support me in equal measures. But I have line managed difficult staff and seen many turbulent line manager relationships in school. It is painful to watch and no one ever benefits.

It is the job of both parties to make the relationship work and, like all good things, it can take some hard work to do so. A little hard work, deep discussion and quality planning and the appraisal and performance management process can be a really useful and productive one. Once you get that right then everything runs more smoothly in schools. If staff have direction, challenge and support then everyone flourishes and we can all focus on what is really important – the students. Having clear direction and ensuring you are working on yourself and your areas for improvement, as well as being secure in your strengths, will ensure that you are performing at your best when the inspection team rolls in.

Putting it into practice

- **Meeting time**: Line management meetings can really make
  a difference to how you manage your work and develop as a
  professional, if you take full advantage of them. Get a time
  pinned down when you and your line manager can meet in
  peace once a week and get it in the diary so you are not used
  for anything else in that slot. Begin the meeting with a brief
  summary of what has being going on over the week to get your
  line manager up to speed. I always advise ensuring that you have
  a standard set agenda so that both you and your line manager
  have a routine of discussion topics so nothing gets missed. It is
  always a good idea to go prepared with a list of questions for your
  line manager drawn from your work in the past week and what
  you envisage will crop up over the coming week.

- **Targets**: Obviously, some targets will be dictated to you and
  centre around data expectations, usually linked to whole school
  data targets. The other targets should be negotiated between
  yourself and your line manager. When you are setting your
  targets make sure you have detailed discussions with your line
  manager about how you will be able to show you have achieved
  these targets. Make the targets challenging and routed in your
  genuine areas for development but make sure you also make
  them achievable. Have your progress against these targets as a
  regular discussion slot in your meetings so that both you and
  your line manager can focus on ensuring you are supported to
  best achieve the set expectations.

- **Blowing your own trumpet**: When you achieve something,
  make sure you let your line manager know. We teachers can be
  coy beings and we must learn that in our job if we don't share our
  achievements then very often no one will know about them or be
  able to benefit from your expertise. When you have a great lesson,
  have positive comments from students, staff or parents, create a
  resource that is well received, have a great set of results from a
  class test or work with a colleague on something of note, make
  sure that you share this with your line manager and celebrate
  these successes. Line managers really do want to support and
  celebrate your achievements as they are also achievements for

them too if they are supporting you as they should be. Blow your own trumpet if you have a good tune to play.

- **Shaping your role**: Make sure you put forward your ambitions for yourself as a teacher and/or leader when you are planning your year ahead with your line manager. This will mean some thinking and consideration on your part outside of your line management meetings. Come to your line manager with ideas as to what you are interested in or they will shape your path for you – which is fine if that is what you want, but just be aware of this.

- **Learning from your boss**: Whether your line manager is similar to you or very different, there is much you can learn from them. They have often been in your position, and may have a different perspective on issues you may be dealing with due to their experiences. It is in your best interest to form a good relationship with your line manager as a colleague and a person so that you can gain the most out of your performance and line management process. Value their input and ask for their advice – that is what they are there for.

- **Observations**: Very few of us relish observations; in fact most of us actually dread them. They can reduce the most wonderful of teachers to quivering wrecks. We must learn to take observations by the horns. They are a chance to show off our teaching. Yes, you will spend longer on the lesson plan than normal, but this does not mean you are 'being fake' it just means you are trying to be your best. Each time you plan in depth as you do for observations you learn more about your own teaching, so relish the chance to develop yourself. Be you, plan and deliver an engaging and developmental lesson for your students and enjoy the ride. If it goes wrong, it goes wrong – take the advice given and work hard to be better.

- **Professional development**: Keep a close eye on the courses that are out there and available for teachers. There are so many great courses on offer that you are spoilt for choice nowadays. (There are also a lot of really poor ones so be mindful and look at reviews if you can.) Generally good quality ones are the Teaching Leaders, Future Leaders, SSAT or Dragonfly courses, among others. I have been lucky enough to be supported to take part in courses provided by all of the above through the schools I have worked in. I make it my mission to ensure that I use the learning I undertake to directly improve my teaching or approach to my role as soon as I am back from the training. This makes me gain the most I can from the CPD but also ensures the school knows I appreciate their support. Some schools and academy chains run their own in-house programmes which are of high quality and these should also be taken advantage of where possible. Search for a course that will develop and support you in your teaching or leading and discuss the benefits of the course with your line manager – you deserve to have training and the school will benefit.

Inspection connection

Ofsted will scrutinise the performance management and appraisal procedures and look over records in an anonymised format. They want to see how well the school is 'developing its middle and senior leaders' and what is the 'impact of professional development on teaching.' They will be looking for good practice and teachers developing themselves professionally.

They may choose to meet with groups such as NQTs or middle leaders and ask about how they are supported and developed in the school. It is a great idea to have things ready to talk about with the inspection team to show how you have developed as a result of the performance management support you may have had from your line manager, or opportunities you have been given to lead any staff training. They will never be privy to the meetings you have so share the good things that go on in your school.

Things to think about

- **In primary schools:** With leadership structures being much smaller in primary, you will need to think carefully about how to progress in your job if this is what you wish to do. Taking on voluntary responsibilities to show off your skills is a great way of standing out from the crowd and being noticed as having potential in a smaller school setting. If you want to be part of the leadership team or have an interest in a particular curriculum area, make sure your SLT know. Be proactive and find good training courses to further your own development.

Make links with other primary schools and teachers in roles you are interested in. Keep your own records and evidence of your progress and work, this will make your end of year appraisal much easier and keep you focused on your performance management targets.

- **In secondary schools:** Be mindful of your development and which direction you want to go in. There are varied routes you can take to develop your career in secondary. Consider whether you want to remain in a subject role, move towards pastoral or perhaps teacher development. Don't be pushed into a certain role if that is not the direction you want to go in.

Developing your practice

Start to look ahead to what you want to do next – even if it is a few years ahead and only a glimmer of an uncertain idea right now. Once you have a rough idea of what you might like to be doing next, discuss this with your line manager. Start to look for opportunities that will develop the skills you need for the role well in advance. Small voluntary projects or larger paid responsibilities are both valuable and should be grasped with both hands – just make sure they are all leading towards your own self-development and that you are enjoying the ride.

Note of caution

Don't expect your line manager to constantly organise you or your role because if you do then a micro-management situation is likely to ensue. Don't blame them for the short falls in your approach to your role. We have to take responsibility for our own development and ask for what we need. Discuss issues and problems with your line manager openly and ask for advice. If they don't help you then fine, blame them, but don't expect them to be psychic; remember we are all human.

Online resources

- Line management meeting agenda
- Year planner pro forma
- Line management meeting notes page

19

Student voice

'Sometimes people don't want to hear the truth because they don't want their illusions destroyed.'

Friedrich Nietzsche

Ask your students regularly for feedback on your lessons: what works for them, what they enjoy, what challenges them, what they find hard and what they feel doesn't work. This can be hard with some classes, but it is a must. Other people in school will be asking them, importantly when an inspection is taking place, so you may as well get their view and work with it. Gather this feedback from self-reflections in exercise books, perhaps after units of work, or use a quick online feedback tool such as the polls in Edmodo or sites such as SurveyMonkey that are freely available. This way you can see trends across the class and over time and save all of the information easily to discuss with the class.

Students will not always know what is best for them in the classroom, but if they don't appreciate why they do certain tasks or are asked to do things a certain way, then they will not gain as much; explain it to them. Having open and honest discussions about learning and teaching will build trust between you and the students. Ofsted inspectors will be speaking to students about their experience in lessons and so should we!

Putting it into practice

- **Questionnaires**: Regular questionnaires are a great way to gain an insight into what your students are feeling about the topics, learning and lesson content. You could choose a few lessons over the course of the term and give the students a satisfaction questionnaire to fill in, much like the questionnaires that are often handed out at the end of a training course. You could base the questionnaires on completely different types of lessons to get a feel for which types they enjoy more. You could also use the questionnaires in similar lessons spaced across the term, tweaking your approach each time in line with feedback from the questionnaires. It will make the students feel valued and it will also make you consider how you are approaching lessons with a view to improvement. You can do this on slips of paper or even set up a www.SurveyMonkey.com questionnaire to collate the responses electronically. You could also use the polls tool in www.edmodo.com and collate the responses in a forum where you can share results easily with your students and parents, as well as get immediate, live results in the lesson.

- **Self-evaluations**: At the end of each topic or unit of work it is always a good idea to conduct a student self-evaluation. This task is focused on the student work and how they have performed, rather than your teaching as such. However, this can reveal a lot in an indirect manner. Students will need training to do this well – I often start by providing sentence starters and examples of responses from 'past students' for them to understand what I expect from them and their responses. Reflecting on the topics, tasks and learning they have undertaken can reveal misconceptions and strengths that otherwise would perhaps have gone unnoticed. This is a great tool for you and interesting to share as a department too if you are all studying the same topic at the same time.

- **Student focus group**: Gather a group of students from your class or classes, whichever is appropriate or would be more helpful. Have a set bank of questions printed out on small cards and get them to talk around the table about each topic in turn.

You should stay out of the discussion as much as possible so as not to guide the debate or influence their responses. Visual prompts or props similar to those used in lessons as discussion aids may be useful to support certain questions you pose to the group. You could have a sixth former, a teaching assistant, a responsible Year 6 student or a student from another year group acting as the prompter, prepared by you in advance, if you feel this might work better. Hosting a student focus group can be fascinating. Students are much more candid with one another and, at the end of the day this is what you want. We can't live in denial about what our students think and feel about our subject, classes and teaching. If we are all open we can move forward together.

- **Informal feedback**: Gathering informal feedback is easy and takes no extra effort or planning at all. Simply make sure you ask students individual feedback questions as you circulate and work with groups or individuals in the classroom. Making sure you note down the informal feedback is important though. We are so busy that it is easy to forget the details of what students say, feel and think in response to our questions. Have a note book or an electronic file open for you to jot down any informal feedback from students. Students love it when you mention something they have said to you a few weeks back about their learning or the lesson – it makes them more willing to engage in talk about lesson and learning if they know you are mindful of their words and that they can have an impact.

Inspection connection

Ofsted clearly state that they will draw 'on pupils' … views to inform inspectors' judgements' so we need to ensure that we already know what those views are and that we are acting and teaching with them in mind everyday. That does not mean pandering to every request that is put in for more cake on the lunch menu or non-uniform days once a week, but it does mean that students need to be listened to and their views respected and represented in their school.

Ofsted will talk to students about their everyday experience of teaching and learning, behaviour and their general school experience. The more we do this in-house with our students, the more they will be able to articulate this to the inspection team. Just as Ofsted will, we need to be paying attention to the 'views expressed by pupils' and addressing misconceptions that are often present when the exploration and open discussion of student voice is not a focus. Don't see student complaints and concerns as the enemy, they are there to be addressed and explored in an open forum. If they are listened to and have a voice then the school is theirs, not just a place they visit.

Things to think about

- **In primary schools:** Younger students can be just as insightful as older students – sometimes they are probably more insightful than the older ones as they are less guarded. Engage them in serious discussions about their learning and let them know their views are valued and it will go a long way to getting them passionate about their work in school.

- **In secondary schools:** Secondary students can be very emotional beings, what with all those hormones racing around their bodies, and this may well come out in their feedback. Don't disregard their remarks just because there may be an emotional tone to it or you don't like what they have to say. However hard it is to hear, sometimes we need to know how these emotional beings view us and we need to adapt. We are the adults and it is our job to do the best we can to make it work, regardless of the type of students we find in front of us.

Developing your practice

Get the students involved in designing the student questionnaires, polls and evaluations. They could formulate the questions for you, plan out when they should take place and collate and feedback the answers to you. They could even present back to the class about proposed changes as a result of their feedback alongside you.

Note of caution

Don't make drastic changes based on one student's feedback. Sometimes students negative comments simply need to be discussed and the issue explained rather than a full overhaul of your practice. Similarly, their positive comments too can be confused with what is actually having an impact with students. A discussion about the reasons behind certain effective tasks that are less popular and slight tweaking may well do the trick.

Online resources

- Student self-evaluation template
- Student focus group discussion cards

20

Balancing act

"Happiness is not a matter of intensity but of balance, order, rhythm and harmony."

Thomas Merton

One Christmas holiday many years ago, I remember leaving school with a pile of books under my arm. I spent the first few days of the holiday marking the books to within an inch of their lives; noting every spelling, error and possible suggestion. Following this less than festive start to my holiday I sandwiched in a couple of days with family and friends before spending the last few days of the holiday planning my lessons in over-the-top detail for the first three weeks back. Upon my arrival back at school I was exhausted from all the work I had done and so was an absolute misery with staff and students alike. When I gave my marked books back to my students they spent less than a minute looking through them and showed minimal interest in the marking I had lovingly slaved over. When I began teaching my ultra-planned lessons I realised I had pitched them wrong and had to rework them all to suit the class better. To summarise – precious holiday time was wasted due to working hard but not working smart. I had not valued the most important thing in this crazy job – my sanity and time to recoup.

Teaching really is the best job in the world but it can drive you to the edge of reason if you let it. Making sure you get the balance right is a constant must for teachers and we regularly need to make sure we are keeping it in check. Too many friends and colleagues have fallen into the trap of not being able to keep the balance. Being prepared is important, but make sure you give yourself time to rest and relax. Having this balance will mean your day-to-day job is easier and you will be in a much better place when the inspectors call. We are the most important resource in the classroom and we need to be able to keep doing our jobs well enough. Teachers, we can do this!

Putting it into practice

- **Daily plan:** Try sitting down somewhere quiet at the start of each day and setting ten minutes aside to think and plan through what you would like to achieve that day. Writing it down in a list is a good idea. The tasks of the day may be gathering lesson resources, setting up an activity for a lesson, marking a set amount of books, catching up with a certain pupil, contacting a particular parent, responding to a staff request or sorting out an area of your classroom. Whatever you need to achieve that day, list it and plan the best way to approach these activities so that you can save time and get as much done as possible. Doing this will help you focus on what is important and what can wait. It will also take away that horrible feeling we all have sometimes – 'I'm sure there is something I am supposed to have done today.' Just check the list.

- **Daily reflection:** Take ten minutes at the end of the day to reflect on how everything has gone. Again, find a quiet place where you will not be interrupted so you can really focus. Think through what has gone well and what you have achieved as well as where it could have been smoother. Were there any parts of the day where you felt panicked, flustered or rushed? If so, then how can you avoid that happening in the future? Even if you are not sure how to improve, think of an alternative approach that may work and give it a go. Doing this is quite settling at the end of a busy day. By forward-planning for future situations you will be relieving the stress of repetitive negative situations and the feeling of hopelessness that accompanies it. If you get into the habit of starting your day by planning out what needs to be done then this is even more useful.

- **The students:** Remember why we are doing this crazy job. Enjoy the fact that we work with young people. It is a privilege to be a part of a person's history and to see them grow and develop through the years. Appreciate the wonderful children that you work with and let them know it; tell them how much you enjoy being a part of their day and helping them discover new things. A little love goes a long way.

- **Rest**: I always try and leave my work at work so that I can focus on things I choose to do when I am at home. For many reasons, some cannot do this and have to bring work home with them rather than stay at school. Wherever you choose to do the work that spills over from the working day in class, make sure you have a set point to stop. I mean it! A wise man once said to me 'a teacher's work is never done' and this, my friends, is a fact. We could always be doing more tweaking to a lesson plan, deeper marking of student work or adding more to the reports we have slaved over. You need to make the decision to stop and stick to it. Put the work away, out of sight, and breathe. Have a bath, eat dinner with your family and put your feet up. We will never be able to do our best if we are exhausted – give yourself a break and *regularly* enjoy your time off.

- **Laughter:** Laughter is the best medicine for most things. Share a joke or a funny story from the classroom with a colleague (we have enough of them!) and just have a good old belly laugh. It makes the world feel like a better place to be and it is scientifically proven to make you feel happier. Laughter changes what is happening in your body: it stimulates circulation, aids muscle relaxation, fires up and then cools down your stress response and increases your heart rate to make you feel relaxed and happy. Everyone is a winner.

- **The real world:** Make sure that you keep connected to the real world during term time. This may sound ridiculous to a non-teacher but we all know how all-consuming school can be during term time. It is important to make an effort to maintain regular contact with family and friends despite the pull of school and work at home. We need a support network and should not let our jobs eat into this. You will be a happier and healthier teacher and able to deal with much more in school because of it.

Inspection connection

There isn't one – this is about you not them!

Things to think about

Both primary and secondary teachers face great pressures in their jobs and should ensure that they make time for themselves and their loved ones. We are in this together. Support one another and congratulate colleagues when they venture home before five one day in the week rather than watch them leave with suspicion and a tut. Speak to one another about how you've enjoyed your free time and encourage others to do the same. We feel guilty enough about the fact that we are doing a never-ending task in teaching and sometimes it takes a colleague to say 'go home and enjoy yourself will you?!'

Developing your practice

Prioritise your time in school to work efficiently whilst you are there. Whenever possible you should keep your work at school and keep your home life as a precious and valued space. This allows you to really switch off and be rested and ready for the next day at school. Obviously this is not always possible but when you can, do so.

Note of caution

Don't let things slip because you need rest time. If the essential workload associated with your job really is too much to manage, speak to a positive, trusted colleague or your line manager to get tips on how to manage. Don't be fearful of asking for help. It is better to ask for help early than to struggle and become ineffective in your role.

Online resources

- To do sheet
- Daily reminders

Part 2

Around the corner

Overview

So, the call has come in. Ofsted are on their way. Your headteacher or most senior staff member available will have spoken to Ofsted on the phone. The senior team will have been called in to meet with the head for a debrief. All of the staff in your school will then be called to a meeting where the announcement that Ofsted are coming will be made. The headteacher and senior team will outline their expectations of students and staff and usually offer words of wisdom and advice on how best to use your time before the inspection team arrives.

The senior team will pull together all the documentation they will need to present to Ofsted and prepare for anything they feel will be a focus for the inspection team. Middle leaders will rally their team together, supporting anyone who needs it and making sure their area of the school is ready. Teachers, this is your time to regroup, focus and get yourself sorted before the inspection begins. Look over your timetable, gather your resources, tidy your room and ready your mind and body for the visit. Your focus should be on teaching great lessons and being the best you can be for your students. That is it.

This section aims to give you quick tips to put in place and use when you have just been told that Ofsted are coming. Central to each chapter is the classic 'to do' list, which will guide you through the final checks and tasks you need to do to be fully inspection ready. For each chapter I provide a 'quick fix' for those who are really pushed for time and a 'going the extra mile' idea for those who are a little more prepared. It is important to keep the students and their needs fully in focus during this time so I have also included some student considerations for you. Again, I have included highlights from the key Ofsted documents linked to the different topics being covered (and the references are also included online). It really does become clearer as the links are being made that if you do your very best and keep the students, evidence and data at the heart of all your choices, then you are on the right track.

21

Observations

"Genius makes its observations in short-hand; talent writes them out at length."

Christian Nestell Bovee

To start off this section, a note on observations in general, whether it is Ofsted or another member of staff. I never felt like I was one of those young teachers that could just go into the classroom and 'wing it' with a smile and a story. My first PGCE observation was a catastrophe. Blind panic meant that I could not remember most of my lesson and I ran out of material halfway through! I ended the lesson a quivering mess, wanting the ground to open up and swallow me. I have since been graded outstanding in observations many times when gradings were the done thing, including by Ofsted themselves. More importantly than that though, my results and the progress my students make over time show that what I do day in, day out works in my classroom and that is good enough for me.

Observations can be one of the most stressful parts of our job, but we need to conquer this enemy. An observation can be an opportunity to show off the very best of what goes on in our classrooms every day. It should not be a one-off lesson where we do what we would never normally dream of doing. But it may well be a little different as we want to show off as much as possible overtly rather than weaving it into the lesson subtly as we do everyday.

Use the advice in this chapter to help with any of the observations you might have, but right now, use it to get yourself in the right frame of mind for the inspection that is now around the corner.

To do

☐ **Prepare yourself:** If you are not on form for the lesson observation you will not be projecting your best side. Start off with a positive mindset: whether it is a fellow teacher or an Ofsted inspector, with the right preparation, you can do this.

☐ **Set up the room:** Check that you are happy with the seating plan well in advance and do not make any last minute changes on the day as this can cause anxiety for some students which is the last thing you want in an observation. Ensure that the tables and chairs are positioned so that all students can see the board without obstruction and that you and the observer can move around the room easily and freely. Position any resources in an easy-to-access place so that there is no fuss during the observation. Be mindful of any lighting issues that could obstruct sight of the board: it is devastating when a lesson loses impact due to the glare on the board. Sort out those bedraggled displays at the back of the room and make them look loved once more. Being in a room every day can make you unaware of some of the things a visitor may pick up on – look at your room with fresh eyes a few days before and get everything in order before the observation.

☐ **Keep it simple:** When you plan your observation lesson don't fall into the trap of making the lesson so complicated that you need a compass, map and a secret code to 'get' what you are doing in the lesson. The activities should all link to the objective and build towards the progress you want to see at the end of the lesson. Keep it simple, keep it focused on what you want to achieve, and make it interesting. Don't over-complicate things.

☐ **High expectations:** Whether you have the struggling bottom set or the high-flying top set, make sure your expectations are always high. Half the battle with students when it comes to progress is their own self-belief. If they get even an inkling that you do not believe they can achieve highly, then they will not work half as hard as they don't see the point. You need to pitch the lesson appropriately so that all in the class can access it while structuring the lesson in a way that will allow them to aim as high as they can. Raise the bar and they will reach for it.

☐ **Planning documents:** All schools will have their own planning requirements, so make sure you are following these. As a basic rule of thumb, providing an outline of the lesson which highlights the lesson objectives, activities and their focus, adjustments made for your SEN, PPG and EAL students, assessment objectives and links to prior and future learning, will be useful for the observer. It is also a very good idea to have a seating plan with student's names, working levels and any other relevant information mapped out on it for them to look over. I also like to provide a data sheet or mark book so that progress over time can be looked at as a snapshot for the class. These documents should not be 'for the observation' but part of your normal planning so it is no laborious task to prepare them. Have them in a neat folder clearly labelled and leave them on the desk where the observer will be.

☐ **Check learning:** Make sure that you have pencilled in regular opportunities to check the learning and progress of the students during the lesson. This may look very different for different teachers, subjects and students. Whether you use a mini whiteboard, clever questioning or some other way of checking, make sure you do it. After every check take a moment to see if you need to provide assistance to particular students, stretch others or go slightly off the plan to ensure they are where you need them to be. Never leave this until the end – it is too late to intervene by then and the opportunity to learn has been missed.

☐ **Enjoy it:** You have worked hard to prepare the lesson and you know your class well – enjoy showing what you are made of. Go in with a positive attitude, greet your observer warmly, and go for it!

Inspection connection

Ofsted have varied their approach to observing lessons when they are in for an inspection now. They may only spend a few minutes in a lesson, spend 25 minutes or more in one classroom or track a group or class of students for an extended period of time to 'assess their experience of a school day' depending on what they are looking at. You may not be observed at all as they clearly state that they do not always have the time to see every member of staff. This is why it is so important to have your good practice routines in place and not panic yourself into doing things that are out of the ordinary. Do what you do and do it well and it will shine through.

Ofsted are not looking for a certain type of lesson or learning when they are in your classroom but that 'pupils' engagement, interest, concentration, determination, resilience and independence – may be seen or be expected to be seen in a single observation.' You will have your own style and approach and as long as this has the student at the centre of it and works for your students then it can't be bad.

In terms of feedback following an observation, if the observation is joint with a member of SLT in your school, then feedback will be given by the SLT observer. If you are observed by just an Ofsted inspector they will generally 'provide an evaluation of strengths and areas for improvement to teachers at programmed times.' They will not provide a grade for your lesson or quality of teaching as they used to. Your observation is used as part of a body of evidence to form a view of teaching and learning across the school. You may be fed back to alone or in a group. Be sure to take the compliments, and take any areas for improvements as useful steps rather than criticisms. None of us are perfect!

Quick fix

Use what has gone before. Think about the journey the students have been on in recent lessons. Think about a lesson that brings together the learning they have done and really ties it all together. Use routines you already have in place with your class in terms of marking and feedback, behaviour and lesson structure to avoid the dreaded 'we never normally do this!' Lever in small sparks of surprise rather than spending hours planning a brand new type of lesson.

Going the extra mile

Using seating to enhance the learning can make a real difference to the lesson outcome. Plan carefully when you are arranging the seating and make sure you use this in the lesson to your advantage, such as directing certain levelled questions to different ability groups or setting differentiated tasks according to the audience on a certain table. It is important to highlight and explain this practice in your lesson planning document so the observer can watch as you pull out the very best from different groups of students.

Student considerations

Make sure you think about the students' experience in the lesson you have planned. Lessons can often go wrong if teachers fail to consider the students' experience of the tasks, teaching and learning. Think through each stage of the lesson and imagine how it will be received by the class and the individuals within it. Close your eyes and imagine the lesson playing out, put yourself in the students' shoes and tweak the things that you think may not work.

22

Lesson planning

"No matter what people tell you, words and ideas can change the world."
Robin Williams

Consider who you are teaching on the day/days of the inspection. Visualise your day. Think about how your students are at different times throughout the day. You know your classes so make sure you avoid common pitfalls you are aware of. If they respond well to upbeat activities in the morning or writing tasks more in the afternoon then make sure this is what you plan. Keep the endgame in mind when planning. Keep the skill you want them to have improved upon at the centre of your planning process. Decide where you want them to be at the end of the lesson, in terms of knowledge and skills, and work backwards from there. Shape all of your activities around building towards the endgame step by step. It is great to think up fun and exciting activities for your lesson, especially if you know you have visitors, but just make sure they are leading the students to where you want them to be at the end of the lesson.

Ofsted clearly state that they do not look for one particular style of lesson and that they don't necessarily require to see a lesson plan when they arrive in your lesson. They may not want to see a plan but they will be looking for an excellently-planned lesson, that is for sure. If you choose not to provide a lesson plan just make sure that the aim of the lesson, its direction and the learning that is happening is obvious. You can decide what works best for you, but I would always advise you to have a lesson plan printed out. Find a lesson plan format that suits you and use it as often as possible – not just when you are being observed, even as you get more experienced! Make sure the plan isn't overly lengthy or the inspector will probably not look at all of it. Keep it simple, to the point and explanatory: for example you could highlight why you will ask key questions, focus on certain groups or use particular resources.

The to do list below includes all of the areas Ofsted will be expecting to see in your plan and the lesson they observe, so make sure you've got them covered!

To do

- ☐ **Class profiles:** Have your class profiles out when you are planning and really use and reflect upon them when you are deciding your lesson objectives, differentiation, resources and lesson activities. Note on your lesson plan when you are addressing the varied needs of different groups within your class. Highlight when you are differentiating – whether it be through questioning, a task, an outcome, resource or activity – so that it is clear to the inspector.

- ☐ **Resources:** Ensure that your resources are all available and ready. Print off everything you need and place them neatly labelled in the classroom where they will not be disturbed. That way you will not be running around or rifling through piles of papers on the day of the inspection. Be mindful not to overdo the resources as less is often more: make them simple, clear and useful.

- ☐ **Differentiation:** Ensure that you have thought out exactly how all students who are EAL, SEN, Pupil Premium, disabled and gifted and talented are being supported, stretched and challenged in your class. Have activities, questions or extra responsibilities ready to challenge your gifted and talented students in the lesson. Have resources, activities or alternatives ready for your students that may need more support than others. Ensure that your classroom is set up in a manner that allows any students with a disability to access the lesson as any other student would. If you are using a lesson plan document then you can just highlight in brackets where you are supporting these groups of students. On your seating plan you can have a brief explanation of how grouping is organised to support these students in their learning.

☐ **Progress checks:** There was a period in teaching when progress checks began to look very stilted and actually often halted the learning rather than spurred it on. This does not need to be the case. Progress checks are essential in lessons in order to ensure that you actually know where your students are and alter your teaching to allow for learning to take place there and then. Once the lesson is over it is too late! You may use something as simple as random questioning to check where students are in the learning you want them to have undertaken. However you do it, make sure you are doing this a couple of times throughout a lesson and adapting how you approach the rest of the lesson or activity with this in mind.

☐ **Literacy and numeracy:** Make sure that, wherever possible, you are weaving in activities linked to the lesson's learning that address these key areas of the curriculum, be it simple or rather more complex. Again, if you are using a lesson plan document then you can very easily highlight where you are doing this in brackets and bold to ensure that the observer can pick this up easily.

☐ **Knowledge:** Consider the new learning students are experiencing in your lesson. Will all students come away from the lesson having been stretched and challenged by what you have taught and the lesson you have planned out? Clearly highlight what skills and knowledge you are covering in the lesson in your planning documents as well as in the lesson itself. It may be that you are building up their competence or agility with a particular skill or body of knowledge – this a great, just make sure it is clear to you, the students and the observer.

☐ **Marking and feedback:** Marking and feedback should be well evidenced in your students' books. Be ready for the inspector to look at books during the observation. Have a certain colour pen that only you mark in so that it is clear where you are marking and where students may be self-correcting or peer marking. It makes it much easier for an outsider to see the process. You could consider including some marking and feedback reflection in your lesson. If you choose to do this then make sure you have trained the students in this skill. If it is too early on in the year to have trained them but you still want to include this, then you might want to break the marking and feedback skills down and teach them a small element of how to reflect on your marking and feedback so that they can grasp it well. Don't expect them to be good at doing the entire thing straight away. Model what you want them to do, show them excellent examples, support them as they do it themselves and ensure they are acting upon that feedback straight away. Having a structured sheet, perhaps in a jazzy colour, that guides them through the reflection and the subsequent task to act upon the feedback, can really help this process.

☐ **Homework:** Make sure that you consider your setting of homework. Do you have a whole school timetable that staff follow? If so, double check when your homework setting slot is and make sure you follow it. The homework needs to be matched to students' needs, and the necessary support or challenge that you provided in the lesson also applies to homework. Link the homework either to what you have done in the lesson or what you are covering in the next lesson. If you are not setting homework you could simply remind students in the lesson when their homework will be set to show the observer that you have not forgotten.

Inspection connection

It is so important to ensure adequate differentiation for all students in every lesson because that is what we owe the students. Ofsted will be looking for evidence of whether 'the most able are stretched and the least able are supported sufficiently to reach their full potential' so plan it clearly into your lesson and make it visible. If you are setting homework or collecting it in during the planned lesson, then make sure you take the opportunity to discuss this clearly with the students and how it is relevant, as Ofsted will be looking for evidence that it is 'appropriate' and set in order to 'match the students' needs accurately'.

Quick fix

If you already have great resources ready to use for your lesson, then use them and enjoy. However, if you do not, then please do not try to reinvent the wheel for all of your scheduled lessons over the inspection period – there really is no need! There are so many great websites out there that offer teacher-created resources for free, and many allow free adaptation after downloading, such as www.tes.co.uk. Make sure you look to see whether someone else has already created what you need. You may well need to tweak it but that should be all at this stage in the game.

Going the extra mile

If at all possible print off the resources, lesson plans, seating plan and class profile in colour to show any colour coding and detail. The codes you use in your lesson plan to show SEN, EAL etc. could all be in different colours to make it easy to track where you are addressing these students' needs. The resources have much more impact if you can see the colour and images clearly as an observer. Money and budget is a barrier to doing this all the time, but for special lessons and occasions it makes for a more polished finish.

Student considerations

Make sure that when you are planning you keep your class in full focus. Think about what they have responded well to in the past, when they have had lightbulb moments or progressed exceptionally – what did you do well then and can you emulate that success now?

23
Data

"What seems to us as bitter trials are often blessings in disguise."

Oscar Wilde

The inspectors will be expecting you to know your classes well in terms of them as people, as well as the data that forms their background, present activity, and future aspirations. Data used well is a powerful tool. Used badly it is a waste of time and can lead to inappropriate pitching of lessons and interventions. Making sure you have the correct data for your classes is essential, so if you are not sure where to find this then make sure you ask the question – and fast!

All schools will have different ways of tracking students and using data. This is fine, Ofsted are not looking for one particular way of you using data and tracking your students' progress. They want to see how you monitor how well your students are doing, and what you are doing to make sure you are addressing gaps, supporting some students and challenging others. When it comes to examination year groups, you will obviously be using examination marking criteria to mark and feedback to students so this makes data presentation easy. With the removal of National Curriculum levels in other years we are facing more of a challenge. However this is also an excitingly freeing time and many schools are formulating their own systems. However you are tracking and monitoring your students, just make sure that you show this system to the inspector. Remember, they will have been informed of whole school polices and practices in this area.

To do

- [ ] **Accurate data:** Extract the most recent data from a reliable source for all of the classes you are due to teach over the course of the inspection. Don't just rely on your old paperwork – double-check and make sure you have everything in order before you start your planning. Has anyone new started in your class since you last formed the class profile? Is there a recent assessment that they have completed that has not yet been added to the class profile? If you have an your assessment coordinator, they should provide you with the most recent assessment data for your class. This should clearly show levels and progress. As well as your data, your assessment records should be ready with your APP data (assessing pupil progress), whichever system your school uses, up to date and easy to access.

- [ ] **Class profiles:** Update the class profiles for all of the classes you are due to teach over the course of the inspection. Class profiles should ideally have assessment data as well as SEN, EAL, PPG and first language data to aid your planning. Have you looked at your seating plan recently and checked that you have students grouped as you want them? Do you want to move them now to reconsider your justification for grouping in your planning documents? In primary your class folder might also include medical information, a list of children who have free school meals and any IEPs.

- [ ] **Printing:** Print off the class profiles for all of the classes you are due to teach over the course of the inspection. Ensure that each one is clearly labelled and formatted for easy reading. Someone who does not know your class will be looking over them so they must be user-friendly. Is there always a queue for the printer in your staffroom? If there is then quickly find a quiet spot in school, log in and get sorted in peace.

- [ ] **Teacher folder:** A great idea is to form a teacher folder as you prepare for the inspection. This could contain anything you like, but should hold what is necessary for all of your lessons during the inspection process – clearly labelled with dividers if possible. Don't be tempted to pull the old sticky labels off a tatty folder knocking around in the back of the cupboard in your classroom – go all out and treat yourself to a new one from the stationary cupboard. It will make you feel organised and well presented. You can have this folder open to the correct class during each lesson and direct the inspector straight to the documentation when they arrive – stress-free for you! Don't overfill the folder; keep it clear and simple as the inspectors will only want to glance at it. The contents could include: lesson plans, copies of resources, class profiles, seating plans, behaviour records, interventions records, prior observation feedback and your assessment records. A great tool for both the inspection and for general use.

☐ **Planning:** As I've mentioned, use *all* the assessment data in the class profile folder when planning your lessons for the inspection. Plastic wallets make the folder a little more professional so use them if possible. This teacher folder is useful for general planning routines, not just an inspection, but if you don't have one then now is as good a time as any to sort one out.

Inspection connection

Ofsted want to see that teachers and leaders alike are clear about where the students are, how far they have come and what we want them to achieve. Using accurate and clear data on your students is one way you can show the story of your students. Inspectors will be looking at trends across the school, but if you have a story worth telling then you should absolutely show it off to the inspection team if they arrive at your classroom. They want to see 'pupils' academic achievement over time, taking account of both attainment and progress' so if you have some great success stories, then provide the data in a simple format and tell the story.

Quick fix

Whether your school uses SIMS/CMIS, Phoenix, Integris™ or any other electronic system to house your data, there is usually a function within your datasheets to enter your reports in the programme and simply add more columns of information. Then you can very quickly export the whole lot – hey presto, you have a ready-made class profile. Columns you want to include are: assessment data, SEN, EAL, first language, FSM, gender, tutor group and prior data such as SATS or GCSE results, if you have access to this information. It saves you searching around and is very simple to update in the future.

Going the extra mile

If you have time, create an enhanced class profile. Consider adding columns that show behaviour points, rewards points and interventions you may have put in place. A one-stop shop for all your student information and a really useful planning and reflection tool for your class – during the inspections and in the future.

Student considerations

Students should know their current working level, how far they have progressed and where they are heading. If you have not already worked this into their learning then think about making a part of your lesson focus on this to ensure that they are up to speed. It is obvious that our students are more than mere numbers and facts on a spreadsheet, but this information can really help with planning, marking, classroom interactions and teaching. Students in primary should know their targets or at least where to find them and what they mean. Targets are meaningless if the students do not understand them.

24

Resources

"Sometimes when teachers use loads of stuff in lessons I get confused and forget what we are doing."

Year 6 student

Resources can make or break a lesson. Too many resources and you, the students, and the visitor will simply get confused and learning will be lost. Inappropriate resources can ruin a good lesson as they become a distraction and students focus on the wrong thing. The key is to keep them simple, focused on the learning objectives and targeted towards the endgame – where you want the students to be at the end of the lesson. A simple image added, word underlined and made bold or a change of font can do a world of good to a previously boring and overly complex resource.

To do

☐ **Lesson plan documentation:** If you choose to use a lesson plan, make sure that you have enough detail to explain your activity choices in connection with your lesson objectives, but not so much that it is overwhelming. Check that the document is well written or printed, and clearly laid out. Ensure that you highlight your differentiation towards different groups throughout the lesson and your use of a teaching assistant if you are lucky enough to have one in the room. Which student or groups will your teaching assistant be supporting and what will their role be? Is there a teacher focus group?

☐ **Differentiation:** Ensure that when you are putting together your lesson resources you are thinking about how they will be received by the students. You do not necessarily need to use different resources for different groups within your class, but consider what they may need in order to access the resource as effectively as the other pupils. Could you include a key word definitions help sheet or provide dictionaries for certain groups of students? Could you use images and/or colour to help students decipher difficult texts or ideas without them realising that it is helping them?

☐ **Printing:** The majority of the time we need to be conservative with what we print and whether it is in colour, but this is a special occasion. Treat yourself and print whatever you need in as many colours as you choose, as you would for all special lessons or visitors.

☐ **Equipment:** Make sure that you have a good amount of extra equipment on your desk in the classroom so that you can very quickly sort out any students who are lacking. Of course they should bring their own and I'm sure they will be reminded often, but these things happen. Don't let a lack of equipment spoil the first part of your lesson – just sort it out quickly and have a quiet word with them once the first activity has started to ensure you are reminding them to bring their own. If they are using new or exciting equipment during the lesson, try giving them some fiddle time in a previous lesson or at the start of the session so the students are not too distracted by the exciting new things.

☐ **Spare books:** Don't get caught out when a student proudly informs you that they have finished their book and have no space left to work. Again, you do not want to be wasting your time with this and sending students off for resources, so ensure you have a stock of new exercise books on hand to quickly sort this type of situation out without any fuss. Ask the student to copy over the details from their previous book and get straight on with the activity. Disaster averted.

Inspection connection

When it comes to outstanding teaching, the Ofsted criteria specifies that they are looking to see that 'all teachers have consistently high expectations of all pupils. They plan and teach lessons that enable pupils to learn exceptionally well across the curriculum.' Showing a well-ordered and clear classroom environment, documentation and lesson is all part of that picture.

Quick fix

Group all your resources, along with your copy of the lesson plan for each lesson, in a plastic wallet as you print them off. Lay these wallets out on your desk or somewhere safe in your classroom in the order in which you are going to teach them so you can just pick up the folder and go on the ring of the bell.

Going that extra mile

Think about fun ways to personalise the resources you plan to use. Could you include a scenario that involves the names of staff members in the school? Could you incorporate the names of the students in the resources? Primary students in particular love this. Familiar names or people and places can easily be incorporated into a puzzle in a maths lesson, a story in an English lesson or a scenario in a computing lesson.

Student considerations

You could have a tub with essential resources stored in the centre of the table and give students the responsibility of organising themselves if they need something, as well as the task of keeping the container tidy and replenished. Set a time for when they replenish and tidy to stop them using important lesson time. Check the things that cause rows in your class. Primary children always love using the smallest pencil, for reasons unknown, so make sure there are plenty of fresh useable resources on each table.

25

Student books

"Whether you think you can or think you can't, you're right."

Henry Ford

Student books are the easiest way for an inspector or visitor to see what your class gets up to on a day-to-day basis so it is important that they reflect the great teaching you do on a normal day. They will be looking at whether the work set is appropriate, marking and feedback is constructive, and if students are progressing over time. Make sure you form a sense of pride in student books from your expectations, and interact with student books at all times. Making sure you use books well in your lessons over the course of the inspection is a must. If you are not using them in the lesson, prepare to have them out for inspectors to see.

To do

☐ **Book covers:** Make sure the outsides of your books are presentable, and simple things like student name, class group, teacher and room number are filled in. It sounds obvious but I'm shocked at how often I have seen this not filled in. Take out pieces of loose paper and worksheets – they do not look good and indicate a lack of organisation. If have not already covered books in sticky back plastic and you have some lying around, perhaps grab a small group of students and get them to help you cover the books for a small reward. It makes them look professional and neat.

☐ **Marking and feedback:** You simply must have your marking and feedback up to date. Sit with the books in a pile, lock the door and get marking. You don't need to mark everything; focus your marking for impact and select what you look at in different pieces of work. Marking the same piece of work in all the books in one go saves time as you get used to what you are looking for. If you have any electronic marking that you do in your classroom, make sure you spend some time printing off what the inspector would need to see in order to show the progress over time that they normally look for in books. Have a file with the printed electronic marking ready for the inspector to look over when they visit your class.

☐ **Ordering:** A simple task that you can do to help aid a swift start to your lessons is ordering your books. This is essentially having your books piled up in the order in which you want them given out. Group books in your pile according to your classroom layout by sticking/drawing a colour or shape for each table or row on the corner of each book.

Inspection connection

The inspection team will be on the look out for evidence that 'assessment is frequent and accurate and is used to set challenging work that builds on prior knowledge, understanding and skills.' The books are a big part of that picture. It is an easy way for an outsider to gain insight into what goes on in your classroom day in, day out, not just in that lesson. They may well collect in books to look over for whole classes or groups of students across the school. They could talk to students about their work to see if they 'understand well how to improve their work ... beyond whether they know their current 'target grade' or equivalent.' So make sure that students regularly reflect and can discuss their achievement in relation to their books.

Quick fix

If you have a situation where you have found yourself falling behind on your marking then prioritise the last few lessons so the most recent work is marked and ready to be looked at. Mark those pieces well. Mark a task at a time rather than a book at a time, by opening all books to the task and piling them up in front of you. When you finish marking each task in each book turn to the next task for marking and form a new open book pile for you to go through once you have finished the first ones – and so on.

Going that extra mile

Any piece of marked work that the students complete to a decent standard deserves a little extra touch – have your stickers and stampers at the ready when you are doing your last marking and make sure you are generous with them if they are deserved. Don't think this is just for the little ones – everyone loves a sticker! It is a good idea to highlight in some way the formally assessed pieces of work you get students to complete every few weeks for the observer, if it is not already. You could simply star the page and write ASSESSED WORK in the corner of the page where this work appears.

Student considerations

If you have updated anything in the student books or marked a piece of work just before the lesson, then make sure that you make the reflection on the piece of work a part of the lesson. This is important in everyday practice but even more so in an inspection. If there is work beautifully marked but the inspector speaks to a student who cannot talk about their feedback or what their next step is, then it is not an ideal situation for anyone.

26

Differentiation

"Everybody is a genius. But if you judge a fish by its ability to climb a tree, it will live its whole life believing that it is stupid."

Albert Einstein

Differentiation is something that should apply to all students in our classes, SEN or no SEN, gifted and talented label or no gifted and talented label. It is anything that we do to help our students learn best. In differentiating, we are teaching to the differing needs of the students in order to allow them to gain the most out of the lesson and move forward in their learning. Once you get differentiation routines into your lessons you don't even think about them, they just become a part of what you do. Sometimes these approaches will be subtle in their nature and this is right in those situations. However, there may be other times when differentiation is overt and discussed with students in order for them to see how and why they are learning something in a certain way, and this too is right in that situation. You do not need to use all possible techniques of differentiation in any one lesson, but at times you may well dip into them all. You need to decide what is best to progress the learning and stretch and challenge all of your students. An inspector will be looking out for the differentiation techniques you use in your lessons. By now you should have your routines set up so it should be quite easy to just show off your differentiation techniques when being observed. What follows are some strategies you could use during the inspection to make sure you have got differentiation covered.

To do

☐ **Starting point:** At the start of a new unit, it is a good idea to start with an activity that gauges exactly where each pupil is as a starting point. This then allows you to differentiate for the individual needs of each student accurately. This can be in the form of a quiz, class or group discussion or a starter activity of some sort. If the inspector is observing the first lesson of a new unit or topic, this is a good activity to include.

☐ **Task:** Make sure you have a selection of different tasks at differing levels of ability to stretch and support where necessary. Alternatively, you could provide the same text to all students but ask them to do something different with it. Think about designing the tasks so that all students can reach a similar point in their learning by the end with no student getting left behind.

☐ **Outcome:** You may choose to differentiate by outcome. Be careful, though, of looking for different outcomes for different groups of students in your class and setting different targets for each student; just because some students are lower ability does not mean you can't push them just as hard as the higher ability students.

☐ **Content:** You could provide different content for some students during the lesson. The resources you give to certain students may be more complex than ones you choose to give to others. Just be sure that all content given out challenges every student. Don't dumb it down but rather open up challenging topics to all students. If you are giving an 'easier' text to some students then have challenges ready for those that excel. You could have extension tasks, either generic or topic specific, to challenge all students that move quickly though the task you set.

☐ **Support:** You might choose to differentiate through support for certain groups of students. This could be in the form of supporting resources being available for students to use alongside their work; learning mats, key word lists, extended reading on the topic, dictionaries, thesauruses, sentence starters, etc. Support could simply come from you working purposefully with certain students or groups of students. This could also take the form of teaching assistants if you are lucky. If you do have the privilege of having another staff member in with you to support the students learning, then just make sure that you plan for them effectively and discuss your plan with them before the inspector arrives. It is a travesty when they are underused or not directed in class.

☐ **Pace**: Modifying the pace of the learning for some students is another way you could differentiate in your lesson. You may choose to have a faster pace for certain students in the lesson, providing a structured tiering of tasks for all learning but leaving some out for certain learners so that they are able to complete the task in the same amount of time. You could get those that worked faster and through more content to feedback to the whole class so that all learners can benefit from the faster pace and enhanced content they undertook in the lesson.

Inspection connection

Ofsted are interested to see whether your school is doing everything in its power to enable all learners of all backgrounds and all abilities to do their very best. They will be 'evaluating the extent to which schools provide an inclusive environment that meets the needs of all pupils, irrespective of age, disability, gender, race, religion or belief, or sexual orientation.' You don't have the power to form their view on the entire school's approach to this, but you do have the opportunity to show them how it is done in your classroom and that forms part of the final picture.

Quick fix

Have dictionaries or other support resources already out and in place in your classroom so that students do not have to fuss around in order to access and use them once your lesson has started. There are lots of great generic support resources for all subjects and key stages that can quite easily be printed off and placed on each table ready to help your student excel. If you don't already use them in your lesson, then limit the new support resource to one good one so that students are not overwhelmed and distracted by them.

Going the extra mile

Plan to challenge your top achievers or gifted and talented students to use sophisticated and high-level thinking skills and specific language in their work and class discussions. You could challenge them to get other students in their group using the language you provide them confidently by the end of the lesson too.

Student considerations

Remember that students are one of your best resources in class. You could buddy students up to support one another. If one student in a row is particularly good at a certain skill, you could use them to support others who struggle.

27

Student engagement

"Imagination is not something apart and hermetic, not a way of leaving reality behind; it is a way of engaging reality."

Irving Howe

Engaging students in the lesson is joyous thing to experience when you are teaching. We all want the students to find the love of learning in our classroom. There may be students that just love the subject or topic being taught and that is a wonderful thing too. But when we don't have a sea of eager and interested students sitting before us, we can do things that help spark their interest and engage them in what is being taught.

When the inspection is looming, take some time to think about what you do on a week-to-week basis that really engages your students and decide what you want to incorporate into your observed lesson. This is not about making your lesson into a show but more about allowing your students the best chance to demonstrate what they are able to do with your guidance. A visitor watching your teaching does not know what you know. You know your students and have seen them in many different contexts and classroom situations. You know how they work best and what they respond well to; so show this off to your visitor proudly! This chapter includes some ideas that you can very easily weave into your lesson to improve student engagement if you feel they suit your class and your students.

To do

- ☐ **Evaluating engagement**: Once you have planned out your lessons for the inspection make sure you give yourself time to evaluate when and where you are sparking student interest and ensuring they are engaged in your lesson content and the learning. Are you happy that you have included what you need to get them interested in what you are teaching and they are learning? Have you thought about how the activities are going to be received from their perspective? Is there anything you can tweak to make it even better?

- ☐ **Voice**: Use your tone of voice to spark interest. We are often unaware of the pitch and tone of our voice in general. It is amazing what a varied pitch and tone can do to change the approach a student takes to a topic or task; use volume to create atmosphere or a change in pitch to build tension. Think about where you could use it in your lesson for impact.

- ☐ **Choice**: Give your students some choice in the lesson at some point. Give a little of the power over to them while still structuring the options towards the desired outcome for the lesson. You may give them the choice of who they work with or which task they complete first in the lesson. Allowing some independence while keeping it manageable for you as the teacher will ensure that students feel involved in the lesson as you go.

- ☐ **Stimuli**: If you have time, incorporate some unusual, interesting or thought-provoking stimuli into your lesson. There are many powerful images available online. Find some that are relevant for the topic being covered in your lesson and use them to inspire, connect, shock, spur emotions and create discussion. Music can move the most closed of students to feel unexpected emotion. Use some powerful opera, upbeat classical, powerful ballads or cheesy pop to help open up the minds of your students to the topic you are teaching. It could be the lyrics, speed, sound or emotions that are the link to the learning. You could reveal the link or get the students to guess how the track is linked to the lesson.

☐ **Challenge**: Lever in enough challenge in the lesson at different points so that all students are kept on their toes. You could have challenge questions or tasks at the ready, or even displayed around the class, that help move the learning on in the lesson.

☐ **Failure and success**: It is important that students never feel the urge to give up in order to remain engaged. Failure and success are all part of the learning journey. We have to find the time to discuss this with our students and make it a happy part of the lesson. Make it clear that failure is okay in your classroom. Celebrate it as an opportunity to learn and not something to be worried about experiencing. It is important to celebrate success too, but it must be well deserved success and not just a token gesture.

☐ **Controversy**: Including a little controversy in the lesson can really get students interested in a topic. Use a controversial one-sided statement and overstate your agreement with it to get the students riled up and debating a topic. This is great fun to do and really gets them talking.

Inspection connection

Remember that Ofsted are there to find the positives in your school and lessons. When they are judging behaviour as outstanding they are looking to see students showing a 'thirst for knowledge and understanding and a love of learning' like we all do. Create opportunities for students to actively participate in the learning process. Challenge them, allow them to lead, and encourage their discussion and ideas even if they take you in an unexpected direction. It is all part of the fun of teaching.

Quick fix

If you can think of a lesson when your class were really engaged and on board with you, then tap into it. What went well? What made the students really connect with the learning? Can you bring the learning from that lesson into this one? Can you structure your activities and the learning in a similar manner? Use what you already know about your class to get them engaged.

Going the extra mile

This is not for everyone, as some teachers wish to be completely private and if that is you then fair enough. However, opening up a little of yourself to the students can really engage them in the lesson – it makes you more real. Sharing a personal anecdote that is related to the learning that will be taking place can really inspire them to become involved and form their own experience to share with others.

Student considerations

Make them care. If they don't care about what you are teaching them they will not be engaged. There is aways a way to inspire them and spark their interest so find it. Take a few minutes to think about your students (you know them well) and what they love and care about and incorporate this into your lesson in some small way.

28

Showing progress

"If there is no struggle, there is no progress."

Frederick Douglass

A few years back I was asked to run a session for an INSET day on 'Progress for Outstanding Learning'. It got me thinking about the tricky issue of how a teacher can get students making real tangible progress and also show that progress is taking place. I researched and mulled over the issue in great detail in the two weeks leading up to the session and gathered together far too many ideas! I have it drilled down to four key areas that help me focus on progress: lesson objectives, progress checks, marking and feedback and success criteria. I hope this helps you too.

It really is all about progress over time rather than a quick fix and a trick levered into the lesson, but there are definitely things that you can do in a lesson to demonstrate you are gauging the progress being made and ensuring all the students are going in the right direction. It is too late to fix it once the lesson is over and the learning is done so it is important to be thinking about this all the time for every lesson, inspector or no inspector!

To do

- ☐ **Lesson objectives:** Lesson objectives are the foundation blocks of learning. If you get them wrong and build your lesson around a dodgy lesson objective the whole structure will collapse. The lesson will not work as it should, it needs those strong foundations to stand firm and tall. Skills-based lesson objectives make it easier to show how students have moved on. You could have lesson objectives that they choose from at the start, all from the same skill but tiered in terms of difficulty. Discuss this process with the students. Always keep the objectives focused and at the centre of all the activities you set up in the lesson.

☐ **Starter:** Include a starter that tests the lesson objective skill in order to show where they are at the start of the lesson. This makes it much easier to show progress to you, the students and the observer. You could have a simple question as a starter for the student to reflect on, a puzzle linked to the skill they will be looking at, a discussion task, a card sort activity with some cards blank for their own ideas or a quiz. Just make sure it is relevant and that the students understand the relevance to the learning and the lesson.

☐ **Plenaries:** Include mini plenaries intermittently, to remind the students how well they are doing, refocus them on the objective and plan for further progress. These should be clearly pointed out on the lesson plan. Mini plenaries do not need to be a massive break in the lesson; a simple Q and A session or thumbs up, middle or down – something like that to bring it back to the lesson objective skill in some way. A good plenary allows the teacher to clearly see who has moved on and who needs more help. This should form the basis of planning for the next lesson.

☐ **Judging progress:** I simply do not believe that a teacher 'just knows' when students are progressing, we are not psychic. (Well most of us aren't anyway!) It is essential that we actually dip in and check the learning is taking place. We also need to check where the students are within that learning so we can adapt what we are doing for all students. For me it is not good enough to just leave it until I mark their books to see if they 'got it' – the learning time has gone then, it's too late. Using some great AFL techniques throughout the lesson is a perfect way of gauging where the students are in the learning.

- ☐ **Progress chat**: Some teachers feel that students won't know if they have progressed and would certainly not be able to articulate it. If this is the case in my class I feel like I have failed. I immediately go back and look at how I can help my students see the steps for progression in this area. Empower them, they need to take charge of their own progress and need us to show them the way. They need to be able to be self-reflective and understand the journey they are on and see the route to the final destination.

- ☐ **Success criteria**: Providing students with success criteria for tasks before they begin is so important. Some students will not need it and will get the right ideas from the outset, but others won't. Don't take the risk that some students will get the wrong end of the stick and be working hard towards the wrong goals – it is so demotivating if this happens. Be clear about your expectations, show examples and show them what success looks like.

Inspection connection

The Ofsted outstanding criteria for teaching in a school states that they are looking for 'sustained progress.' That is progress over time not in 20 minute slots in a lesson. Of course, students will show clear progress in some lessons but in others it is part of the journey towards progress. Bring the students in on this knowledge and allow them the skills to recognise and appreciate that progress is not linear and not always quick. That way no one will feel confused or cheated in a lesson.

Quick fix

If you have time for nothing else, work on your lesson objective. Make it skills focused and manageable yet challenging. Make this the centre of everything they do in the lesson. The starter activity should show where they are beginning. Pinpoint slots in the lesson where you can see and show how far they have come from the start of the lesson. End the lesson with a final progress check.

Going the extra mile

You could bring in, as a part of your lesson, a reflection slot on their previous learning on the same or a similar and linked topic. Linking it to their prior achievements and struggles can help students progress in their learning in the present lesson, because they feel they are continuing their learning rather than embarking on a brand new struggle.

Student considerations

Half the battle with students making progress is their lack of self-belief. They have to believe they can achieve and trust in us that we are there to guide them. I care a great deal about getting the very best out of all of my students. If my students don't do well, I always look to myself before pointing the finger at them or their past performance. Regardless of whether they are top set or bottom set, I ensure they all know that I believe they can achieve and will fight to get them to do so.

29

Your classroom

"Only put off until tomorrow what you are willing to die having left undone."

Pablo Picasso

I cannot emphasise enough the difference a tidy, organised and attractive classroom can make to the success of an inspection. Walk into your classroom with fresh eyes and look at it as a visitor will look at it. It can be easy to become oblivious to the pile of old display materials that have been heaped up in the corner, the torn and tatty posters on the back wall or the wobbly chair in the middle of the room. Sorting the room out and showing it off really does make a difference to students' attitudes to learning, your happiness day-to-day, and an outsider's perspective when they visit your room. This is something you should be on top of throughout the year, but now you know the inspection is imminent it is time to make sure your classroom is in the best state it can be!

To do

☐ **Tables and chairs:** Do a sweep of the room and check that there is no graffiti on the tables. You could get the cleaners to come and help you out – they have superpower cleaner that will get rid of it in seconds. Go to every chair and give it a shake to check that it is not wobbly. If it is then we all know that it is highly likely to to become an unnecessary distraction and source of hilarity in a lesson. Swap any wobblers for more stable ones from a less-used classroom or communal area such as the hall for the sake of your sanity over the course of the inspection. Finally make sure that there is a clear flow around the classroom, even when students are in their seats. You should easily be able to get from the door of the classroom to any point in the room without having to climb over a table. I know that lots of us are pressed for space, but small tweaks can easily open up a classroom. If you know that your classroom is cramped then consider whether you can change the position of any of the chairs on certain tables, or move a table up against a wall to allow for some more space.

☐ **Board and interactive whiteboard:** Make sure you give your whiteboard a proper clean, not just a wipe to add to the weeks of grey smudge on there. Get a little board cleaner and it will look more professional – also your scribblings of wisdom will look much more important to your students. Check that your interactive whiteboard pens are all present and correct and not squirrelled away in your pencil case or down the back of your drawer. If your whiteboard benefits from calibrating then make sure you do this so that it is all aligned and ready to be used. If you need to manually adjust the focus, colour and projection on your interactive whiteboard, then this is the time to do it. Don't leave it slightly to the left with a green tinge as it has been for a couple of weeks. Get the focus, projections space, and colour all sorted by adjusting the dials on the projector so you are ready to go.

☐ **Health and safety:** It is very important that health and safety has been considered in your room. Look for any pieces of carpet that may have come loose, ceiling tiles that are slightly shifted, windows that slam or fire exits that may be obstructed. Let the caretaker know immediately if there is anything that you cannot sort out yourself so that you need not worry about it on the day.

☐ **Shelving and storage:** Take a look around the room at your shelving and storage units. Start with the open shelving and ensure that there is some order to it. Stack books up as they should be, place boxes and files neatly in order and organise the student exercise books for easy access. Is there anything that is just piled up on shelves and hasn't been touched for years? Can it go in the bin to clear some space?

☐ **Lighting:** Check the lighting in the room. Are there any flickering lights that could cause a distraction or headache? If so, then get the caretaker onto this quickly so that it can be sorted. If you are lucky enough to have a bright sunny day on the day of the inspection, then consider not using the fluorescent lights and ensure all blinds and curtains are fully opened to allow a natural and less stressful light into the classroom.

☐ **Equipment:** Conduct a stock check of all essential equipment: spare pens, pencils, rulers, rubbers, a hole punch, stapler, tape, exercise books, paper and anything else you use regularly. Also ensure you have a clean board rubber and board pens in a few colours. Make a visit to the stationary cupboard and stock up.

☐ **Titles:** Check all of the displays in your classroom and the surrounding area have clear titles, so that it is obvious to someone else what you are actually displaying. One clear and large title stating the key concept/topic and a selection of smaller subtitles can really bring a display to life. This does not take long and makes a big impact for students and visitors alike.

☐ **Borders:** A display without borders looks a little sorry for itself. Make sure that the display boards in and around your classroom have clear, fresh and well-attached borders. It takes two minutes to pop a new one up so do this if necessary. A professional look about the place makes everyone feel better about being there.

☐ **Blank display boards:** Scour around your classroom and nearby corridors to ensure there are no sneaky blank display boards. Now is the time to pop up some subject-specific images, a course outline, exam tips or something else quick and useful for students. Make sure the place represents you and your students well.

☐ **Tatty displays:** Double-check all your displays in the classroom. Are there any tatty pieces of work hanging off the wall by a single thread that need pinning back on or replacing? Is there a particular display board that has faded terribly and is so old that is has become irrelevant? Could any of your displays use a few related colourful images? Now is the time to get all your displays shipshape.

- [ ] **Tatty walls:** Are there any walls in your classroom that have a serious case of peeling paint or staining? If so, make a beeline for the site staff and ask if they could splash a lick of paint on the offensive section of the wall. If this is not an option then cleverly position a poster or display until you can deal with it at a later time. It is easy not to notice these things in our own rooms.

- [ ] **Corridors:** Don't neglect the corridors around your classroom. The site staff will undoubtedly be doing last-minute jobs so let them know if you spot anything out of place or untidy, as they could be able to save a little time.

Inspection connection

Ofsted say that when they are judging behaviour and safety in a school they will take into consideration 'pupils' respect for the school's learning environments.' If it is clear that the environment in which students are learning (your classroom) is a place where they want to be, they understand the routines and structures and they can navigate around and use well, then this is partly addressing these concerns. It is also a much nicer place to work!

Quick fix

If you have any closed cupboards or filing cabinets in the room, now is probably not the time to get into a spring clean as they are not on view, but do make sure that they are organised enough to close correctly and don't make the room look messy. However, if you or the students access a cupboard in the room regularly during lesson times and people see into it, then this cupboard needs to be sorted in the same way as the shelves.

If you are short on time and have a really tatty display in your room, then don't spend time taking down each piece of work and all the backing and boarders – just pop up some backing paper over the old display and it is as good as new. No one needs to know!

Going the extra mile

If you can make time quickly put together some labels for different areas of the classroom where things are stored. You could have labels for groups of class books, stationary and different tables names. Cover them in sticky back plastic and place them where the items can be found – the room immediately looks more organised and inviting.

Think about having a colourful and interesting name display for your classroom. Perhaps you want to share your favourite book, quote or silly fact about yourself. Print a poster outlining who works in your room and a few facts about them – interesting for students and visitors to look at as they enter.

Student considerations

The students will respond well to a healthy overhaul of their classroom and the hallways. A tidy, colourful and well-organised classroom equals happy and focused students, which is just the attitude you need them to have for an inspection (and every other day of the year!)

30

Your role

"You are braver than you believe, stronger than you seem, and smarter than you think."

A. A. Milne

When Ofsted are in, it is very common for groups of staff, such as NQTs or middle leaders, to be called in for a meeting with the inspectors. If this is the case, then it is much better if you have taken a few minutes to reflect on your journey so far and what you want to go on to achieve. What has the school done to support you, etc? It makes for a much better and a truer reflection of what is going on in the school if you have prepared this. It will avoid those regrets: 'I wish I had said that …'. Every meeting, lesson observation and event that goes on in the inspection helps form a view of the school, so make sure you are doing your part for the school.

Knowing your role within school and what you have done to progress since you took it on is an empowering thing. We often do not spend enough time dwelling on our role, our achievements and our targets, but spending time doing this really helps you feel a renewed sense of purpose and direction in your job. The students are the centre of what we do and should also be at the centre of your targets and aspirations for your role. Be the best you can be so that you can help them to be the best they can be. Get a notebook and jot down your reflections so that you are clear about your personal professional journey.

To do

☐ **Job specification:** Ideally you will have a professional development folder where you collate your achievements towards your goals in line with your job specification. If you do not have this then search out your job specification. Take some time to think over your role in terms of: what you came into the role expecting to do, what the role has become, and how you would like to develop the role further. As a teacher, what have you worked on developing within your own practice this year or in recent years, and what has been successful? If you lead an area then you may be called upon to talk about your role, and share successes and the areas you are still working on. Knowing your job specification well and what you have done in line with this is a great help in aiding discussion with inspectors.

☐ **Performance management targets:** Have a look over your performance management targets from last year and at present. Which courses have you been on to develop towards your targets? Are there any projects, small or large, that you have undertaken to address issues raised within your targets? Which trials have you got through in your teaching that have added skills in line with your targets? Have you organised or helped organise anything inside or outside of school that has moved you towards achieving your targets? Have your worked with another member of staff to help them to improve, and has this allowed you to achieve your targets? Make sure you acknowledge your achievements and note them down so that you can easily share them if you are called upon to do so. Be proud of your professional achievements.

☐ **Your achievements:** Have these clear in your own mind. Whether you are a teacher, head of department or deputy headteacher, you will have things that you have struggled with, and reflecting on how you overcame these struggles will turn them into positives. Share your struggles if you feel able to, as others can learn a great deal from you. Have you overcome a struggle with differentiation in a mixed class, behaviour management with a particular student, public speaking in assemblies or letting go of the reins and letting the students lead the learning? It is a powerful thing to know your weaknesses and celebrate overcoming them, and it will give you confidence on the inspection day.

☐ **Your areas for improvement:** Whilst celebrating successes is vital for continuous improvement, one must also know the weaknesses within. No person and no school is perfect, so don't be fooled into thinking you can sing your own praises without being honest with yourself. Discuss the areas that still need improvement with your line manager, team, and as a whole school. There is no shame in this so long as there is work going on to address these areas.

☐ **Your aspirations:** Knowing your aspirations in terms of your career and professional development, and a timescale for achieving them, can give you a real sense of purpose in your day-to-day life. Whether your aspirations are to become an expert in an area, or your own teaching, or senior leadership, know where you want to go. Know what you are doing right now to put yourself on the path to your dreams. If you are a leader meeting with the inspectors, then this is useful in helping you focus on the things you do that make a difference – not only to progress you and your development, but also the school and the students.

☐ **Your line manager:** Find a few moments to check in with your line manager in the lead up to the inspection. Check that there is nothing that they need from you or that it is essential for you to prepare. Give them a brief rundown of what you have done in preparation. If you are a line manager, then make sure you check in on those you manage with words of encouragement and support to rally them along. Don't add to their stress at this point! We all feel the pressure but must be mindful not to project this onto other people – seek support instead.

Inspection connection

Ofsted will be interested in investigating 'the effectiveness of the support and professional development put in place for NQTs and other teachers who are in the early stages of their careers' as well as teachers at other levels in the school. The senior leadership team will, of course, be discussing this at the top level, but your experience and how you have developed is important to the inspectors too. We do a tough job, us teachers, and we are generally very good at supporting one another. If you don't show off the positive opportunities and support you have had, then they won't know.

Quick fix

Get your job specification and performance management target document printed out, and simply make brief notes in the areas around the typed words. Use the documents to guide your thinking and form a spider diagram of reflections around them. Keep everything in one place if you need to save thinking time.

Going the extra mile

Think about displaying some inspirational quotes about overcoming struggles and aiming for the very best in everything that you do. There are loads of free sheets online that take no time to find and display. This will keep you positive and focused and motivate your students too!

Student considerations

Instilling focus and a drive for improvement in your students is essential. They need to see where education fits into their lives and futures, which will motivate them to do better. Share some failures you have overcome and successes in your life and career to empower them.

31

The team

"The miracle, or the power, that elevates the few is to be found in their industry, application, and perseverance under the prompting of a brave, determined spirit."

Mark Twain

Whether you are part of a small or large team, leading or being led, it is important to rally together at this time. When the inspection is announced it is crucial that you hatch a plan so that you all come out of the inspection happy with what you have done and how you have supported one another. Put any differences aside and really pull together – it will make a huge difference to how you all cope and feel about the whole experience.

To do

☐ **Support staff:** Make sure you have had a catch up with any staff that will be in your room supporting you over the course of the inspection. Brief them on what the lessons will involve and make clear how you need their help. They may well have suggestions themselves, so make sure you consider these too and alter your plans where necessary. Try to make a slot the night before to meet them if you can, or at least before school starts if that is not possible.

☐ **Colleagues:** Are you a part of a subject, department, leadership or year group team in school? If so, make sure you check in with whoever leads that team so that you are aware of any issues or events that are cropping up over the course of the inspection.

No one needs surprises while the inspection is in full flow and it is easy to forget things you wouldn't normally.

☐ **Positivity:** Things can all feel a little overwhelming when the inspection call comes in but it is important to put things into perspective. There is only so much you can do, and that is what you will do. Working as a team will speed things up and make the experience more manageable. Make sure you and your team remain positive and think of solutions to any issues rather than waste time moaning. No school is perfect – make the best of the great school you have and be proud of what you do well.

☐ **Morale:** Remember that in the lead up to and during the inspection everyone will be under pressure. This makes it even more important to make sure you say hello in the hallway, smile at people, offer some reassuring words, thank people, and explain yourself clearly to avoid misunderstandings. If you don't, then morale will very quickly spiral downwards and the atmosphere will be unpleasant. Don't wait for someone else to start the ball rolling – get out there and boost the morale of your team, and yourself!

☐ **Teamwork:** Make sure you work together. Are there a few jobs that you will all be doing? Are certain people faster than others at some jobs and is it possible for you to divide up the workload to get things done quickly? Work with each other's talents and get things done together. If someone is suffering more than everyone else then make sure that the team rally around that person and buoy them up. You are all in it together and a team is only as strong as its weakest link – we all have a responsibility to help one another become stronger.

Inspection connection

The inspection team want to see the professional support that we give to one another and our students on a daily basis. They state that they are looking for 'an orderly and hardworking school community.' Working together in harmony is what we are all aiming for. We are not always perfect in achieving this, but we need to show off what we are successful at.

Quick fix

Allocate jobs that can de completed in a single hour blitz of the department and classrooms. One person could check furniture and safety and chase up site staff to sort out any issues. Another member of the team could make an essential equipment list, check all classrooms for missing items and deliver new supplies. Someone else could load themselves with displays and a staple gun and quickly refresh the boards around the department as well as stapling any loose posters and displays. These are just a few examples, but you can see how divvying up the jobs could save you all a lot of time and repetition of work.

Going that extra mile

If you know that one team member is really worried about a certain element of their practice, offer them a tip and reassure them that they can do it. Kind words go a long way in stressful situations like this. It will make both them, and you, feel better!

Student considerations

Students seeing a functioning and professional team working to support one another and overcoming their individual differences is one of the best lessons. Whether the staff are respectful and kind to one another or not, the students will follow their lead. Which would you prefer?

32

The students

*"I made sure the students knew in advance we would be having a visitor –
and that there was nothing to be nervous about!"*

Secondary English teacher

The students are why we do what we do. We are teachers and regardless of
an inspection the students must remain at the centre of everything we do.
Don't allow your focus to be clouded because an inspection is on its way.
Inspectors want to see you putting the students at the core of learning,
getting the most from them and challenging them as you always do. Keep
them in focus at all times.

It is important that you make a choice about how you will address
the inspection with the students so that they feel comfortable with the
process too, otherwise anxiety may lead to a warped view of what they
are like in your lessons. They may well feel anxious too, so make sure you
know your classes and prepare them as best you can for the visitors that
you have in school. Remind them that they have a chance to really show
off their school and be proud of what they do everyday too. It is not just
about the teachers. Involve them in the process. You have the power to
create the climate in your classroom.

To do

- ☐ **Honesty:** Although you do not want to put on a show for the
  inspectors, do not pretend they are not there. Make sure that
  wherever possible you have spoken openly with the students
  at least the day before the inspectors arrive about why the

inspectors are coming and what they are looking at – the learning that goes on in class and over time. If the students sense a feeling of anxiety and stress from you, they are very likely to mirror this in their behaviour, so stay, or at least act, calm!

☐ **Reassurance:** The day before the inspection you should reassure the students that they are not about to go into an exam. Yes, they want to present themselves in their best light, but they do not have to put on a show. Even if students don't appear to need reassurance about inspectors coming in they will always benefit from this.

☐ **Appearance:** Check that any school posters or reminders about uniform are clearly displayed in classrooms and corridors in advance of the inspection so that staff and students are remaining mindful. Make sure you impress upon the students the importance of presenting themselves professionally. Tutors and parents and carers should be checking uniform issues and sorting them out – but if one or two slip through the net, pull them up quickly and quietly when you see them.

☐ **Expectations:** Check that your expectations of your students, and those of the school, are displayed somewhere in the classroom. Make sure that you are thinking about the promotion of high expectations with even more vigilance than you normally would. These high expectations should include speech, dress, work, effort, thoughtfulness, manners, participation, interaction, listening and respect.

☐ **Equipment:** We all want students to remember their equipment and to bring spares, but in reality this is not always the case. Keep those high expectations but prepare for equipment loss or breakage and have spares to lend. You could label or sticker them or ask for an exchange of some sort (perhaps their travel pass, prized trinket or student planner) in return for borrowing equipment.

Inspection connection

At the end of the day, Ofsted are there for the students. If they see students misbehaving, being disrespectful and not focused on learning then we have failed. They will be looking at whether there is a clear 'adherence to school uniform policies' and we need to ensure that we are doing our bit to support this effort. They will be interested in whether they can see that teachers 'set out clear expectations for pupils' behaviour' in our classrooms and around school. When it comes to outstanding teaching they are also looking to see evidence of 'consistently high expectations of all pupils.' We would be wrong to disagree with any of those things being observed in our school as we want the best in this area too.

Quick fix

Arrange it so that any equipment you may have to lend or give out during the lesson is in an easily accessible place where it will not have to be shifted around or get lost. If this is done the night before then you will not need to think about this during the lesson, and it can avoid time-wasting and possible conflict.

Going the extra mile

Have a special greeting posted on your door so that your students enter feeling welcomed. Again, this is not something you have to do from scratch, as there are plenty of free images, posters and quotes online. It makes the entrance to lessons that little bit more positive.

Student considerations

It is *all* about them!

33

Your health

"To keep the body in good health is a duty ... otherwise we shall not be able to keep our mind strong and clear."

Buddha

Be kind to yourself. Looking after you is of paramount importance when the inspection bell rings. If you are not on form then all your hard work over the school year with these classes, and over the course of your career, can go unnoticed and overlooked. All the inspectors will see is a flustered and stressed out you and that is no good for anyone. Don't wait until you are stressed to try and relax – be preemptive and look after your stress levels before they take control of you. Stress can be beneficial and spur us on if we control and channel it. It is important to be self-aware and notice stress rising in our bodies and minds, and respond to it.

To do

☐ **Relaxation:** Just taking five minutes alone in a quiet place and focusing on your breathing, being peaceful, or looking at an image that you like, is a great way of relaxing when you are stressed. If you find this challenging, explore the many relaxation recordings available free on the internet. A good place to start is YouTube or Vimeo and just search relaxation/meditation. Choose a length of recording to suit your requirements and time restraints, get some earphones or a quiet room and immerse yourself. Doubters out there give it a try! Alternatively find your own personal way to wind down like watching an episode of your favourite programme, listening to the radio or having a cuppa. It is tempting to reach for a glass of something cool to take the edge off but remember you need to be at you best the next day so make the right choice for you. It may seem like you don't have enough time for this, but you will make silly mistakes if you are tense and not able to relax.

- [ ] **Stress relief:** You know yourself, so make sure you provide yourself with what you know relieves stressful situations over the lead up, and during the actual inspection. The night before the inspection take time to look after yourself, whether it be a fast-paced run, a bubble bath with candles or to pump out your favourite tunes and have a boogie. Get into comfy clothes as soon as you get home to get you into the right frame of mind and feel at ease. If you still have preparation to do at home then just make sure you have time to de-stress and prepare yourself for the next day so you are in a great place to show off your abilities. If you have a scent you like, then have this scent on a tissue in your pocket during the inspection – when you feel stressed, close your eyes and sniff your scent-infused tissue. You will be amazed how relaxed it can make you.

- [ ] **Sleep:** Really try to get enough sleep the night before an inspection. Running on adrenalin alone will make you ill and probably make you look ever so slightly crazed – don't freak your students and colleagues out! Know your own needs. If you have trouble sleeping try out the apps and free recordings available on the internet that are designed to help. Read a book, have a warm drink and relax. You need to recoup.

- [ ] **Family and friends:** If it helps then call, text or pop in to see a family member or friend for ten minutes, have a chat and a hug. You need to focus on work but if seeing or hearing them helps you work better then make the time. The people who know you best will know what to say to make you feel better and believe in yourself. Let them know what you are going through and let them support you if they can. Have a laugh with your partner, best friend or family – it can be a great tonic to stressful situations such as this.

☐ **Self-belief:** You are not being asked to do a circus act during the inspection (unless you teach circus skills!), you are being asked to teach. This is what you do every day and you know what you are doing. Be proud, be thoughtful in your preparation, but at all times believe in your own ability, training and experience. You can do this. Tell yourself this confidently a few times in the mirror.

Inspection connection

This is about you and not them!

Quick fix

Make sure you eat a healthy and balanced diet. You will be able to work a lot faster and more efficiently if you are giving your body and mind the nutrients it needs to work properly. Although the packet of biscuits or bag of jelly sweets may seem like the answer they will cause a spike in your energy levels followed by a serious slump. Look after yourself and eat well so that you are not unwittingly slowing yourself down.

Going the extra mile

On the day and in the lead-up to the inspection make sure you are wearing clothes that you feel professional in, but that are also comfortable. If you are constantly having to adjust your clothes, shuffle your feet in uncomfortable shoes or breathe in because of garments that are too tight, you will not look or feel good. Wear something that looks good and feels comfortable and you will feel more yourself. Sort out clothes for the full inspection prior to the start so you don't have to think about last minute washing or ironing!

Student considerations

If you have an aura of calm inner peace and confidence then the students usually reflect this in your class. Be the person you want them to be in the classroom.

Part 3

Today's the day!

Overview

This section aims to give you some advice and guidance on how to get through the actual inspection and come out the other side alive and happy.

The inspection is upon you and there is no running away. Don't let panic or stress get the better of you. Embrace the inspection and relish the opportunity to rally together and show what you are made of as teachers, team and school. Now is your time to shine bright.

I must reiterate that no two inspections are the same. The inspection team will be looking at different things in different schools and your own individual school set-up will influence how they approach the time they spend on site. However, there is a typical approach to the inspection which is outlined below.

The usual activities that will occur include: lesson observations, meetings with groups of students, listening to students read, student work analysis, looking over school documentation, analysis of staff and Parent View questionnaires, meetings with groups of staff such as NQTs or middle leaders and discussions with governors or equivalent.

The first day of the inspection will typically involve the lead inspector meeting with the headteacher. The inspection team will then plan out and begin observing lessons. The lead inspector will be updating the headteacher on their initial findings as the inspection progresses. The inspection team will usually find a slot to provide feedback to the teachers they have observed. The day is normally rounded off with the inspection team meeting and inviting the headteacher to discuss the day.

The second day usually begins with the inspection team, or a representative, meeting with the headteacher once again. The team will then continue with their planned inspection activities. The lead inspector will meet regularly with the headteacher to share the progress of the inspection. The inspection team will find a time during the inspection process to feedback to each teacher observed. The final team meeting will then take place, with the headteacher invited, in order to discuss and decide upon judgements taking all evidence gathered into account. The day will conclude with feedback being give to the school governors, other senior staff and any local authority or academy representative.

So that is what the inspection team and senior staff in the school will be doing, but what about us teachers? Well, that is simple, we will be teaching. You should definitely know your school's strengths and weaknesses that were highlighted in the last Ofsted report. Remind yourself what they were by looking at the report on the Ofsted website, if you have a couple of minutes. It is important to know what is happening during the inspection so that you can be as helpful as possible, so looking over the inspection checklist in this section of the book will help you think about that. But your main concern is what you do every day – to teach your lessons to the best of your ability and keep the students focused on learning rather than the strange people wandering around their school.

The focus in the following chapters is on cool, calm and collected survival and success when time is no longer on your side. I list the very last checks you should be making in key areas of your life and practice when the day of the inspection is upon you. I have also included positive comments made by Ofsted in their reports on outstanding schools. These schools are from all over the country, and are both primary and secondary. It is wonderful to look at these reports as the teachers were clearly able to show their passion for their job and the students shone.

34

Before you leave the house

"We need to celebrate everything that is good about our education system. We will still be here, even after all the politicians have gone."

@TeacherToolkit

The time has come. There is no more waiting. The morning of the inspection is here and it is time to get your game on. Being on top form in stressful situations does not come easily to everyone so here are some things you can do to help the process along the way before you get into school and the day begins. Some of it might sound obvious, but do take the time to think about these things. Prepare yourself as best you can by having a calm and smooth running morning routine in place. This will help you to get into the calm and content mindset that you need to be in to be ready to face the day.

Last checks

- ☐ **Wake-up time**: Make sure you set a reliable alarm the night before. Set it for a time that will allow you enough time to properly wake up. Those extra five minutes of broken sleep will not make your day run better. Set a second alarm in case you press snooze on the first alarm in your sleep. You could actually place the alarm a little way away from your bed so that you have to get up to turn it off. You will then be able to sleep well secure in the knowledge that you have systems in place to guarantee you will wake up at a good time ready to start the day.

☐ **Food**: Eat a wholesome slow-release breakfast like porridge with nuts and fruit, or scrambled eggs on wholemeal toast. Don't succumb to your craving for a bag of sweets followed by a pain au chocolat. It may seem like a good idea to start the day with a sugar fix but let me reassure you that is it not. If you want to be on top form you must eat a breakfast that will keep you going and stop you running on pure adrenaline and sugar!

☐ **Outfit**: It is amazing how a well thought-out, fresh outfit can make you feel. Hopefully you will have planned your outfit in advance but double check, just in case, that there are no stains or tears. The last thing you want is for someone at school to notice for you!

☐ **Two-minute pep talk**: Take a few moments once you are ready to leave to gather your throughts. Have you got everything you need for the day? Have you said you would bring something in for someone else? Have you got your phone? Have your checked your journey route for any issues? Have you had a good breakfast to get yourself ready for the morning? One last check of the outfit and you are ready to go.

Remaining cool, calm and collected

Find a quiet, airy spot and do some deep breathing; in through the nose and out through the mouth. This can do wonders to relax you and calm you down. It forces you to stop everything and just breathe. Taking deep breaths helps the body take in more oxygen than you would normally and in turn improves your energy levels – who needs caffeine?

What Ofsted said

> 'Students are full of praise for their school. There is real sense of community where all feel valued, respected and morale is high.'

The Sacred Heart Language College (Secondary)

Our students surprise us sometimes when outsiders observe them. We see them day in, day out and sometimes we can miss just how wonderful they really are. They want to be proud of the place they spend the majority of their time too, so have faith and remain positive about and with your students today.

> 'Teaching is of a high standard. Teachers plan very interesting lessons and pupils learn quickly.'

Kielder Community First School (Primary)

You care deeply about what you do. You wouldn't be a teacher otherwise. Teaching is not a job you can just come into every day and sit out. If you don't love it you won't be doing it for very long, that's for sure. It is hard work but it is good work. You teach all day every day so have faith that what you are doing is the best that you can for the students that you teach. Enjoy your lessons today.

35

The journey in

"Success is a journey, not a destination. The doing is often more important than the outcome."

Arthur Ashe

You make the journey in every day so this should be a breeze, right? Don't take this for granted. Make sure you have planned and prepared for your journey. Today is bound to be the day when there are delays or roadworks, so just plan for this eventuality. Don't be tempted to load yourself up with a million things to prepare for the day either, just take what you need and yourself and go on your way with a lighter load. The journey in is an opportunity to gather your thoughts and focus yourself on the day ahead.

Last checks

- ☐ **Your route:** So long as you have double-checked your route and planned an alternative if necessary this should be a doddle. No stress and no hassle!
- ☐ **Music:** Get your favourite music playing while en route to school. It is amazing the calming effects music can have when you are at your most stressed. Get your earphones in or the speaker in your car going and blast out some feel-good songs.
- ☐ **Run through:** Whether you have a car journey or a public transport commute ahead of you, use this as an opportunity

to run through your day. Imagine your day going the best it could possibly go and how that would feel. Imagine yourself arriving and setting up your lessons, tasks or meetings for the day with ease. Picture yourself teaching your first lesson of the day and run through the actual lesson in your mind. How does the lesson work well for you? What is the student perspective of what is being taught and learnt? If you could have done it again, what might you have tweaked? Do this for your next lesson too not leaving out the exit of one class if you are secondary, quick preparation of resources and entrance of the next class. If you are primary then make sure you have planned the journey to assembly or playtime or the transition between activities Can you subtly be getting your next class resources ready towards the end of the last lesson as the students pack up? Run through anything you need to do over your break and in which order it is best to do this. Do this for the rest of your day – slowly running through what the day will hold and just preparing yourself for the day ahead. The same applies to any meeting you are involved in – be prepared and think about what you would like to say or get across during that time. It does not matter if everything does not run as you had planned it in your head, running through your day will make you more able to deal with issues and allow you to confidently tackle the tasks.

Remaining cool, calm and collected

Think of images or metaphors that help you deal better with stress. This may sound a little crazy but it works! For instance, if a problem arises imagine that the problem is a knot; the more you panic and pull in different directions the tighter the knot will become until it is impossible to undo. Another image you could use is to imagine that the problem you are facing is something delicate like an egg, the more pressure you put on the egg, the more likely you are to break it and get mess everywhere which will take even more time to clear up – take your time and handle it with care. Or you could think of a motivational phrase or two that ring true to you and find strength in their good advice.

What Ofsted said

'Teaching is of a consistently high quality. Teachers have high expectations of their students. They use their enthusiasm and excellent subject knowledge to inspire students so that they can make rapid progress.'

Highlands school (Secondary)

Self-belief is so important in life. Remember that our students look to us for validation and when they achieve we need to make sure they know we appreciate it. When they don't achieve, we need to keep them going and hold on to the high expectations that self-doubt chips away at. Always make them believe that they can do their very best even if they are struggling. Struggling is a good thing. The victory that you fight for is always the sweetest.

'Teaching is always good and frequently outstanding. Teachers have high expectations for all their pupils and this is reflected in the quality of learning seen in lessons and in work books'.

Chorlton CofE Primary School (Primary)

Remember that inspectors look at various things to form their view of the school. They are not there to form a view of you as a teacher. You form a part of the picture that they build of your school as a whole. Some of the things they will look at to help them are: students' work, lessons and data. You have prepared your books, planned your lessons and have your data for the class neatly printed out for the inspection team to see. Just do your thing now and teach.

36

Ofsted inspection checklist

"Coming together is a beginning; keeping together is progress; working together is success."

Henry Ford

There is a lot to take in when it comes to the guidance that Ofsted issue. Below are a few of the main things that they will be looking at. The items below are not a checklist for you to tick off in your lesson or meetings with Ofsted but a selection of things they will be discussing as a team for you to be aware of. Remember, this list is by no means how they will judge you as an individual teacher but rather how they will come to a decision on the different areas they assess when looking at all the evidence the gather across the whole school. The checklist is adapted from the outstanding grade descriptors in the school inspection handbook 2015, pages 38, 47, 55, 61 and 71.

Last checks

Quality of education provided

- ☐ The teaching, curriculum, students' attitudes to learning and achievement.
- ☐ The educational experiences on offer and how they prepare students for their next stage of life.

- ☐ The provision in place for promoting literacy and mathematical knowledge.
- ☐ The provision for the students who are the most able, disabled and have a special educational need.
- ☐ How and if best practice is spread and shared in the school.
- ☐ The provision for spiritual, moral, social and cultural development.

Quality of leadership

- ☐ The leadership team's level of expectation and ambition in students and staff and how it is communicated and promoted.
- ☐ The leadership team's understanding of the school's performance, staff skills and attributes and students' attributes.
- ☐ The relationship between governors and senior leadership team within the school.
- ☐ The quality of the school policies.
- ☐ The quality of the professional development provision in place for staff at all levels.
- ☐ The school's curriculum design.
- ☐ The achievement in all subjects inluding English and maths.
- ☐ The school's relationship with parents and carers.
- ☐ The improvements evident across the school.
- ☐ The procedures in place to identify and deal with children who are at risk of harm.
- ☐ The plans, controls and procedures in place for financial management of school funds.
- ☐ The effectiveness of the early years and sixth form provision.

Behaviour and safety of pupils

- ☐ Students' attitudes to learning when working alone, in groups or with staff.
- ☐ Students' attitude to learning across all subjects.
- ☐ Incidents of low-level disruption and how it is dealt with.

☐ Opinions on behaviour in the school from parents, staff and students.

☐ Students' behaviour and attitude in and around the school site.

☐ Students' understanding, attitude and approaches to dealing with bullying.

☐ The effectiveness of the school's strategies to promote high standards.

☐ The improvements in behaviour of individuals or groups with behaviour needs over time.

☐ How safe the students feel in school and what they understand to be unsafe behaviour.

Quality of teaching

☐ The quality of teaching over time.

☐ The progress and achievement of all groups of students in the school.

☐ Teachers' expectations of students.

☐ How well lessons and the curriculum are planned.

☐ How teachers check and respond to students' understanding.

☐ How well literacy and numeracy is planned and taught across the curriculum.

☐ How well staff impart knowledge and the response of the students.

☐ The quality and impact of marking and feedback from teachers.

☐ The effectiveness of teaching strategies including setting of homework.

Achievement of pupils

☐ The progress students make in all subjects including English and maths.

☐ The progress of all students regardless of starting point in comparison to national figures.

☐ The attainment and progress of disadvantaged students.

☐ The reading habits of students in all subjects.

☐ The acquisition, development and application of knowledge of pupils in all year groups.

☐ The learning of groups of students particularly those who are disabled, have a special educational need, are disadvantaged and most able.

☐ The standard of attainment of all groups of students.

Effectiveness of early years provision

☐ The rate of student progress in relation to their starting point.

☐ The preparation of all students for their next stage of education.

☐ Gaps between attainment of all groups of students and national figures.

☐ How stimulating the learning environment is.

☐ How well the learning environment meets the needs of all students.

☐ The quality of teaching over time.

☐ The quality of assessment.

☐ The motivation levels, attitude to learning and responses to staff of all students.

☐ The development of the students' understanding of how to keep themselves safe.

☐ The students' behaviour, self-control, cooperation and respect for others.

☐ The policies, procedures and practices around health and safety.

☐ The strategies used to engage parents and carers in their child's learning at home and school.

☐ The approach taken by leaders and managers in the drive to improve achievement.

☐ The impact of the training and development of staff.

Effectiveness of sixth form provision

☐ The quality of teaching, learning, achievement and attitudes to learning.

☐ The progress of students in all groups including those that are disabled, have special educational needs and are the most able.

- [ ] The degree to which teacher subject knowledge and expertise ensures the needs of all pupils are met.
- [ ] The preparation of all students for their next stage of education or employment.
- [ ] The quality of extension and enrichment activities that students partake in.
- [ ] How much students contribute to the life of the school.
- [ ] The amount of students that complete their study programmes.
- [ ] The achievement and progress in all subjects at all levels including English and maths.
- [ ] The gap between the achievement of disadvantaged students and other students nationally.
- [ ] The standards of attainment and progress of all groups of students and how they compare to national figures.
- [ ] Students' attitude to their learning inside and outside of lesson time.
- [ ] The quality of the careers education, information, advice and guidance on offer.
- [ ] Students' understanding of potential risks to their health and how to manage them.
- [ ] The leadership of the sixth form provision.

Remaining cool, calm and collected

Tell your inner voice to 'shut up!' Sometimes we can be our own worst enemy and allow self-doubt to take over. We all have things that we doubt about ourselves either because we are inexperienced in that area, someone once made a mean comment or just because that is how our mind works. Self-doubt thrives in stressful situations, so make a decision: don't allow it to rule you during the inspection. Be strong and be positive about what you have to offer today.

What Ofsted said

'Teaching is of a consistently high quality. All students are stretched and challenged by the work they are given. Resources chosen to support students' learning are interesting and stimulating.'
Outwood Academy Portland (Secondary)

Make sure that all the resources you use in your teaching are clearly linked to the learning you want the students to undertake. Prepare varied and interesting activities that help the students explore the topic, and ensure every activity and conversation builds some way on the learning objective for the lesson or sequence of lessons.

'Outstanding teaching means that most pupils make rapid progress. Teachers use their excellent knowledge of what pupils already know to plan challenging work for all ability groups.'
Elmore Green Primary School (Primary)

You know your students well, so make sure that you use your knowledge of what they do well and where they need support to push them to the next level in the lesson and their learning. Make links to prior learning, lessons, topics, struggles and achievements to constantly remind them of how far they have come and what they have achieved.

37

Your space

"When adversity strikes, that's when you have to be the most calm. Take a step back, stay strong, stay grounded and press on."

LL Cool J

Do some last-minute checks to make sure your classroom is spotless! You should be able to welcome in the inspector and introduce them to your world with pride and confidence. Students who come into a classroom knowing that the teacher is proud of their space and has taken care and time to organise it automatically have more respect for the space and the teacher alike. The room is a reflection of you so make it a good one.

Last checks

- ☐ **Stand your ground**: Take time to just be in your space before the students arrive, the lessons begin and the day takes over. Stand in the space where you usually stand to introduce your lesson and imagine a great day ahead of you. Think through each of the lessons you will introduce and look forward to them. Imagine the students sitting in their seats enjoying their lesson and getting involved in the learning. Stand your ground with these positive thoughts and banish all worries and negativity about the day ahead. Don't underestimate the power of positive thinking.

- ☐ **Furniture**: Take a few minutes to check over the furniture in the room. Are all the chairs still in their places? Don't wait until the students are in to realise that you are two chairs short and have to delay or disrupt the start of your lesson to sort the situation out. Are all of the tables aligned properly and where you want them? It sounds silly, but untidy tables have a really bad first impression for anyone walking in the room. Is the whiteboard and the interactive whiteboard clearly visible from all seats in the room?

☐ **Lighting**: Check the lights are working well; if they are flickering then make sure that you turn them off as this can be a health and safety risk and can cause distractions and headaches in some students. Is there a time of day when the sun shines directly on the board making it impossible to see? If so, what are you planning to do about it?

☐ **Surfaces**: Have a final scan over the surfaces in the room to check you have not missed anything. If that pile of student work is still on top of the cupboard then pop it away somewhere until you have time to sort it out – not now! What about your desk? Make sure it is tidy and everything looks shipshape.

☐ **Displays**: Look around in wonder at your newly spruced up displays with their neat boarders, clear titles and beautiful colour. Make sure any last minute additions you made last night are tidy and still glued onto the wall!

Remaining cool, calm and collected

Create a calm environment. Surround yourself with things that you know make you feel calm and composed. If you like silence then find a quiet place when you need to keep your cool. If music makes you feel peaceful then keep a set of headphones handy throughout the day to listen to your tunes of choice and have a little bop along to them. If the bright lights in school make you feel the pressure then turn them off and enjoy a bit of natural light instead. Don't give yourself an excuse to feel stressed. Adapt the environment to alleviate as much stress as possible.

What Ofsted said

'Students are very proud of their school. They have very positive attitudes towards their learning. They enjoy school and are determined to do well.'

The Westgate School (Secondary)

Let the love of your subject shine through in your lessons. Students are truly inspired by the passion that they see in a teacher when they are teaching and this passion always transfers to the students' responses in class as well as in their work. If they see that you care then they will care too. If you are positive and enjoying your lesson then the student will too. Even when you are tired and not in the mood to be excited about your lesson, strive to overcome this and let the passion shine through and you will be surprised how energising it is for you too.

'Pupils display excellent attitudes to learning, no time is wasted and much is achieved in lessons.'

Warmsworth Primary School (Primary)

The preparation you have put into your classroom and your resources so that there is no fuss or delay in the learning will help you through the day of the inspection. Having an organised lesson and learning space allows students to progress much faster and focus on what they need to in order to move forward. Allow the pupils to shine today, remember it is much more about them than you in an inspection.

38

Lesson preparation

"Before anything else, preparation is the key to success."
Alexander Graham Bell

This is a vital part of the morning. Setting everything up so that you are ready for the day ahead will make everything easier. It can be the small things you do this morning that will make things run all the more smoothly. Attention to detail can really pay off here. The knowledge that you have nothing you need do bar pick up your next well-prepared resource that is placed just where you need it is reassuring beyond belief during a hectic day. Remember that your role in the inspection is to perform in your lesson so make sure you have everything in place to do that well!

Last checks

☐ **Student books:** Make sure that you have all your students' books stored in the room and easily accessible for the day. You could line up the piles of books in the order in which you are teaching the classes that day so you need think of nothing once the day has begun. You could even sort out your students' books into table groups so that you can swiftly hand them out at the start of the lesson and not have to remember where each student is sitting. Have books on the tables ready for use. Make sure there is no chance of students wandering about 'looking' for resources.

☐ **Student resources**: Are there resources that you will need to hand out to the students during your lessons today? If so, you might want to get them all set up in the order that you want to use them. It is a terrible sight seeing a teacher scrabbling around to find the resources they were sure were just on their table. Get them set up and organised in advance and simply direct a student to the correct resources to hand out when required.

☐ **Electronic resources**: Now is the time to check the computers or devices you might be using with students in your lessons today. If there are some not working, what will you do to allow the lesson to go ahead if the issue cannot be sorted? Check your interactive whiteboard is working properly. Log into your teacher computer and turn everything on; don't rely on the fact it always worked in the past. Load up and look over your PowerPoints if you are using any. Are they all saved where they should be and you have the most recent version? Are you relying on the internet for your lesson at all? Have you checked that any video clips or music you might be using are accessible and work in the classroom? Make sure you check over everything and quickly replace anything that is faulty with a different solution or approach. If something is missing or goes wrong it is not the end of the world – at least you know now instead of halfway through your lesson with a class full of students and an inspector watching!

☐ **Space and resources for your visitor:** Make sure you have a copy of all lesson plans, seating plans, data sheets and lesson resources in one easily accessible place ready for the inspector. A table in the corner of the room is ideal so they can scan over them while you get on with the lesson. Have them well ordered and labelled so that they can be easily looked at. The inspector will probably not look at much there as they will want to be looking at the teaching and learning actually going on. Simple and clear documents clearly laid out for them is best.

☐ **Lesson plans**: Ofsted do specifically say that they are not looking for a particular style of lesson or lesson plan so however you are presenting it is fine, but do present it as it really does help them see the thinking behind your lesson. Take a few moments to scan through the lesson planning documents you have ready for your lessons today. Are you happy with the order of tasks and learning that you have decided on? If not then now is the time to make that last-minute tweak to the lesson format and associated resources. Small changes are fine at this point but do not go for any big changes that you will not have enough time to think through or prepare in time for the day's start.

☐ **Endgame:** When you are thinking through your lesson plans, looking at the tasks you have set and resources you have ready for the day, try and focus on the endgame of each lesson. What is it you want the students to have achieved, learnt or be able to do by the end of the lesson and have you set up your lesson to best allow them to do this? Are the tasks in the lesson all purposeful and aimed at developing skills and knowledge towards the endgame? Keep the endgame in mind.

☐ **Equipment**: Do a last check on the correct lesson equipment being present and correct should be undertaken now. You have just looked over your lesson plans, make sure you have all of the resources you have planned to use. Also check that you have spare essential equipment like board pens, writing pens, pencils and rulers etc. all stored in a place you can easily access them.

☐ **You**: Make sure you are sorted for the lesson. Have you thought through the questions that you want to ask? Have you thought through the questions the students might want to ask you because of the content of the lesson? Remember that the inspector is not the enemy and you just have to be yourself. You can do this, so make sure you build a little bit of self-belief up and enjoy your lessons.

Remaining cool, calm and collected

Appreciate what you have. Rather than dwelling on what you do not have or have not managed to do, instead focus on what you do have and how much you have achieved in the lead up to the inspection (and indeed your career!). Some believe that taking time to cultivate an attitude of gratitude improves mood, energy and well-being. We so often forget how much we have and it is important to refocus on this now.

What Ofsted said

'Teachers have exceptionally good subject knowledge and use this very well to plan lessons that motivate and enthuse students to learn.'
'Teachers mark students' work regularly and provide clear advice for next steps in their learning.'

John Taylor High School (Secondary)

You know your subject well and the students have a lot to learn from you. Use the fascinating things you have learnt during your education and training in your subject area to inspire your students to want to know more. Motivate them to keep trying harder through your comments in books and in person so that they too want to become experts.

'Teachers provide enjoyable activities that are often exciting and make pupils think hard.'
'Pupils are highly engaged by activities in lessons. They try hard and want to learn.'

St Paul's CofE Primary School (Primary)

Keep the challenge high at all times today. Don't settle for anything better than the very best and get the students working hard for you. Challenge and support them in equal measure and get them enjoying the learning that is taking place in your classroom. Encourage and reward those that try hard, it is a great motivator for others to do the same.

39

Whole school inspection

"Never be in a hurry; do everything quietly and in a calm spirit. Do not lose your inner peace for anything whatsoever, even if your whole world seems upset."

Saint Francis de Sales

The list below shows a number of things that schools usually have prepared ready for an inspection. In some cases the inspection team may well have looked at these documents prior to their arrival, if they are available. Some may not apply to your school setting. The list is not there to act as a list of things for you to do, or even things that your senior leaders will be doing the night before, but things that they will have already prepared and want to show and discuss with the inspectors.

Last checks

- ☐ **Previous Ofsted report:** Ofsted will want to be aware of any areas of strength and development that were highlighted in the previous Ofsted report.
- ☐ **Complaints:** They will look at any qualifying complaints about the school. They will not investigate individual complaints but will look into any possible wider issues raised by complaints.
- ☐ **Parent voice:** They will look at all responses received through Parent View (their online questionnaire).
- ☐ **School website:** The inspectors will check that the statement of Pupil Premium is available on the school's website. They will also

look at the general information available, how the site is set up for staff, students and parents, how the curriculum is represented and special educational needs information.

☐ **School RAISEonline report:** RAISEonline provides interactive analysis of school and pupil performance data. It includes data on assessment, attendance and exclusions. The report is produced each year.

☐ **Ofsted school data dashboard:** The data dashboard report provides a high level summary of a school's performance data. It is simple to use and publicly available online.

☐ **Performance and pupil-tracking data:** The inspection team will look at the schools performance and pupil-tracking data.

☐ **Financial records:** They will look at the school's financial records and procedures, including funding agreements.

☐ **Online information:** They will conduct an internet search and look at any information that is in the public domain and reported in the press. They are looking for any possible safeguarding issues that may need to be followed up in the inspection.

☐ **Off-site provision:** They will look at whether the school has any pupils being educated off-site but still on roll. They may assess the quality of that provision for the student and how the school works with them.

☐ **School self-evaluation:** The inspection team will look at a summary of the school's self-evaluation document (SEF).

☐ **School improvement plan:** The school's improvement plan will be looked at alongside the school's self-evaluation document.

☐ **School timetable:** They will look at the school's timetable for all lessons, staffing lists and times for the school day.

☐ **Enrichment timetable or plans:** They will look at the school's enrichment/extension/after-school clubs/school trips timetable and plans.

☐ **School policies:** The inspection team will look at the various school policies that are in place and being followed by staff.

☐ **Record of staff vetting:** The inspection team will look at the school's record of staff vetting and the processes and procedures that are followed for all adults working with students in the school.

☐ **Exclusion records:** They will look at the school's record of exclusions, the reasons behind them, actions taken and any patterns.

☐ **Bullying records:** The inspection team will look at the school's record of incidents of bullying, including those involving racism, disability prejudice and homophobia. They will also be interested in how these incidents are dealt with in the school.

☐ **Safeguarding records:** The inspection team will look at the school's record of reported incidents that were highlighted as possible safeguarding incidents and the actions taken.

☐ **Attendance records:** The inspection team will look at the school's record of absence and how that is dealt with in the school.

☐ **Evaluation of teaching records:** The inspection team will look at the school's record of the evaluation of the quality of teaching in the school. They will not ask to see graded lesson observations.

☐ **Performance management records:** The inspection team will want to look at the most recent performance management outcomes and their relationship to salary progression. These records will be provided an an anonymised format.

☐ **Documented evidence of work of the governors:** They will look at evidence of the work of the governors and their impact.

☐ **Student books:** They will look at a selection of student books or portfolios.

☐ **Student voice:** The inspectors may ask to look at any collection of evidence from student voice questionnaires or meetings. They will be talking with students and be interested to see if the views expressed are the same.

☐ **Staff voice:** The inspection team may ask to look at any collection of evidence from staff voice questionnaires or meetings. They will provide all staff with questionnaires upon arrival so will be interested to see if the views expressed are the same.

Remaining cool, calm and collected

Relax your face and elbows. No really. If you feel your body, or indeed your mind, tensing up during the day then take a minute to just relax your body. Close your eyes and focus on your facial muscles. Let all the muscles in your forehead relax, force them to if need be. Then relax your eyes, cheeks, mouth and jaw one at a time. Keep your eyes closed and face relaxed and drop your elbows like they have a heavy weight attached to them. Remain like that for a minute or two. Most people try and relax from their shoulders but I find relaxing from your elbows is even more effective.

What Ofsted said

'The quality of teaching is outstanding. Questions are probing and the tasks set are imaginative and challenging. As a result students are highly engaged in their learning.'

Harris Academy Greenwich (Secondary)

Questioning is a resource-free tool that you have at your disposal all of the time in the classroom. It is so powerful and versatile. Plan in regular whole class and individual questioning slots in the lesson. Make it fun or serious, complex or simple, open or closed, thought-provoking or knowledge-affirming. Mix it up. You may want to plan a few specific questions that you want the students to get to the bottom of and that are pivotal to the learning you want them to undertake in that lesson.

'Pupils throughout the school, including those who have special educational needs, those who are learning to speak English as an additional language, those who are disadvantaged and those who start at different times, achieve exceptionally well from their different starting points.'

Acresfield Community Primary School (Primary)

Expect the same for all your learners. Provide the resources and support they need to get to where you want them to be – the very top. Make them believe that they can do it, provide the right environment and show them the way.

40

The inspectors

"Nothing gives one person so much advantage over another as to remain always cool and unruffled under all circumstances."

Thomas Jefferson

Ofsted inspectors come in all shapes and forms and with a whole host of different experiences under their belt. Some will be experienced inspectors and others new to the inspection team. They will all come with very different careers behind them but with one thing in common – they all want to make our schools the very best they can be. They do not have an easy job and very often have far too little time to assess a school well. It is our job to make sure they have a clear and accurate picture of our school in it's best light so they can make a fair and real judgement. They are not the enemy and we must not demonise them. However much we do or don't look forward to inspectors visiting they are a part of school life so we may as well embrace them.

Last checks

☐ **Greeting**: If an inspector arrives at your door please do make sure you greet them. Yes it is a nerve-racking experience, but do try not to freeze in horror or completely blank them as they enter as this is just not a friendly greeting. Make sure you welcome them into your room and alert the students to their presence in a calm manner. There is no need to stop the lesson completely and tell them everything you can think of about the unit of learning and the class history, but a friendly hello is a good start.

Encourage the inspector to look at books and speak with students at their will.

☐ **Ready resources**: Once the inspector is in the room you can direct them toward the resources you have ready for them. These resources will be in a place where the inspector can look over them without distraction of other paperwork or resources – a spare table or surface somewhere.

☐ **In-lesson discussion**: If there is a period in the lesson when the students are working independently, you may want to briefly speak with the inspector about the scheme of learning or lesson sequence you are in the middle of to further clarify the resources and paperwork you have provided for them.

☐ **Say thank you**: When the time comes for the inspector to leave the room make sure you thank them warmly for being a part of the lesson. Involve the students in saying thank you and goodbye if you feel it is at an appropriate time during the lesson to do this. Make sure they leave feeling that you are glad of their presence and looking forward to any possible feedback. They are there to help schools improve remember, which is never a bad thing.

Remaining cool, calm and collected

Relax and unwind. Be mindful of muscle tension in your body. Stress affects us all in different ways but most people have a point or a few points that tense up in stressful situations. Sometimes you won't even realise it is happening but it can cause you some really problems and lead to aches and muscle tension. Have a good stretch and loosen up all your muscles. Relax your face muscles too – these are often overlooked.

What Ofsted said

'Students enjoy school. They work with concentration and enthusiasm and are proud of their achievements.'

Sirius Academy (Secondary)

Make sure that you have a clear plan for your lesson (written or not) that has direction and focus but is not too rigid. You need to be free enough to enjoy where the students may take the learning within your parameters. Help them explore the topic you are guiding them through and encourage them to work hard and delve deeper into the topic individually. Praise students who are doing as you would like all students to do and watch others fall into line.

'Teaching has been very effective in motivating and engaging pupils, and has enabled them to make excellent progress from their starting points.'

Curry Mallet Church of England Voluntary Controlled Primary School (Primary)

There are many ways to motivate your students and keep them learning all the while. Think about what inspires the pupils or groups of pupils in your class and use that insider knowledge to shape some of your lesson approach. It is not pandering to them it is letting them know you know them as learners. Students and teachers are all on the same team working together to help everyone improve.

41

Is everyone ready?

"Whether you think you can or think you can't, you're right."

Henry Ford

Everyone will be feeling the pressure right now and they may not all have planned and prepared as you have. If someone is clearly in a flap when you come across them then do your bit, calm them down, reassure them and tell them they can do it. If that is you later on in the day then they can do the same in return. A smile and a quick chat can make the world of difference to both the other person and indeed to you (although you should ensure that you don't let them stress you out! Stress can be contagious so don't catch it – remember, you are ready!)

Last checks

- [ ] **Your students:** The students will feed off the emotion of the adults during the inspection so you need to be as you want them to be: calm, positive and proud of their school. Don't pretend nothing is happening as that would just be strange! Acknowledge that there is an inspection going on but ensure that they know that they are not expected to be performing monkeys. You want them to be focusing on learning, not the inspectors. Greet the students warmly in the morning around school and as they enter your classroom, allay any fears they may express to you about the inspection process and get on with your day.

☐ **Your teaching assistant:** Make sure that your teaching assistant feels supported and ready for the inspection too. You are a team in the classroom. Ensure that they know that. If they have fears and worries then together you should discuss them, rally together and show the inspectors what you are made of. Double-check that your teaching assistant knows exactly what is expected of them in the lessons and why. Run through your lessons with them so they are fully aware of the learning journey from start to finish and can work with you to guide the students easily.

☐ **Your team:** Now is the time to really work as a group to show your team off at its best. This is no mean feat but together it will be easier that attempting it alone. Visit each team member (whether it is your year group or your subject area team) and greet them. Come together as a group if you can spare a few minutes and just reassure one another that this is your time to shine and you will relish it as a group.

☐ **Your leaders:** Don't forget those above you. Don't presume that they feel the pressure any less or more than you do; it is just a different pressure. If you see one of your school leaders over the course of the inspection stop and speak with them. Make an effort to say hello on the morning of the inspection if you see them. They will be very busy just as you are but a friendly face and an quick word is a great way to show a team spirit and will boost morale all round. School leaders at all levels have their own responsibilities that they will be scrutinised for as well as their teaching in the classroom. They may have fewer lessons in your school but no less pressure in this situation. They will be a part of the meetings and interviews with Ofsted and will need to feel support from their team so make sure you show it. If things have gone well during any part of the inspection, make sure you congratulate the leaders responsible for that area of the school. They will do the same if your part of the inspection is a success. Remember that we are all in the inspection together. We work so hard so celebrate when things go well.

☐ **School governors:** The governors are very much a part of the inspection and will be waving their flags in support of the school during the process. The governors work hard to ensure that the school is run well, with the best possible intentions and with the students at the heart of decisions made. You may or may not see them around the school. If you do then give them a nod and a wave.

☐ **The headteacher:** Because we all care about the result our school gets this is a nerve-racking time for everyone, not least the headteacher. The headteacher will be working closely with the lead inspector, getting feedback as the inspection progresses. They will highlight anything they are concerned with in terms of how the inspection is being conducted, and will very much be on the look out for whether everyone in the school is treated fairly and seen in their best light. If you do see your headteacher, give them a warm smile and supportive comment about the inspection. Everyone wants the best for the school.

Remaining cool, calm and collected

Have a good old giggle. Today is an important day but remember it is not the end of the world! Chat with friends and have a laugh about it all. Crack a few jokes and jolly everyone up a little. Share a few funny school or home memories that will keep you all amused through the day. Light the morning up a little and enjoy yourselves. Also, some studies have shown that laughing can reduce certain stress hormones too – bonus!

What Ofsted said

'Teachers gauge the quality of students' work very well, set them challenging targets and show students clearly how to improve their work.'

St Olave's and St Saviour's Grammar School (Secondary)

Keep those expectations high and really stretch and challenge the students in your classroom. Demand the best from them and nothing less. You have your marking and feedback up to date in student books so be proud of it. In the lesson today, can you find opportunities to feedback and give students clear and specific targets to improve their answers to questions or work produced?

'Teaching is outstanding. Letters and the sounds they make are taught exceptionally well by teachers and teaching assistants.'

Stallingborough CofE Primary School (Primary)

Work closely with other staff members in your classroom; remember you are a team. If you and the other adults in the room are all sending out a constant message of high expectations in behaviour and work then the students will know exactly what is expected of them all of the time. Let your teaching assistant into the passion that you feel for the topic you are teaching the class. Involve them in the class dialogue and teaching of the topic. When students see adults becoming enthused they are much more likely to do the same.

42

The moment of truth!

"Keep calm and carry on."

British Government 1939

When the time comes for your class to enter the room there is no more preparation, it is time. Make sure you are focused on them and their learning rather than anything that has led up to this moment. Forget the fluster you got in yesterday over that final resource you were making. Forget the fact that you changed the plenary for this class this morning. Forget the fact that the inspectors are here and could be paying you a visit. It is just you and your class against the world now.

Last checks

- ☐ **Greeting:** Students very quickly pick up on emotions, so if you feel nervous then take a moment and get yourself together before you let the class in. Make sure you warmly greet your class at the door as they enter. A class that feels welcome is much more likely to be on board with you as you start your lesson.

- ☐ **Reminders:** Make sure you don't forget to remind students of expectations as you normally would. Don't see reminders about behaviour, uniform or equipment as a failure during an inspection. Better to preempt any issues by regular reminders than have an issue very obviously crop up during the lesson and a student claim they did not remember that expectation. A friendly reminder and expression of your high regard and expectations of them never goes amiss.

☐ **Rewards**: Rewards are a great motivator for everyone so remember to use them when they are earned. A reward can be in the form of merits, stickers, stamps or whatever else your school uses. It can also take the form of a privilege of some sort or simple praise. However you choose to reward your students just do it. Don't get swept up in teaching the lesson; listen and observe the students and celebrate their successes.

☐ **Sanctions:** Don't ignore any issues that arise in the course of your lessons during the inspection. Don't carry on regardless and hope that they didn't see what just happened. It is not a failure on your part if a student does happen to fall short of your's and the school's high expectations. If an issue with behaviour, attitude, uniform, equipment or anything else does crop up then just deal with it calmly and swiftly. The inspector will be looking to see your approach to such issues and if you deal with this well then surely this is a plus all round!

☐ **Relationships**: Show the relationship you have with your class to the inspector. When a visitor is in the room a teacher, or indeed the students, can clam up and not show how they really are with one another. This is a real shame as it can really show a lot about the teaching and learning that goes on in that room. You are the adult and you create the climate so make sure you ensure that you make students feel relaxed with the fact that inspectors are around. Focus on the students, the lesson and the learning and the rest will fall into place.

Remaining cool, calm and collected

Avoid the 'what if...' thoughts that will undoubtably pop up in your mind at this time. You are right, things can go in a million different directions and you do need to be prepared but there is only so much you can do. Don't worry about all the things that could possibly happen. Prepare a great lesson, make sure your surroundings are clearly organised and attractive, make sure you are well and calm and do what you do – teach. If something out of the ordinary happens, it happens – that's life.

What Ofsted said

'The overwhelming majority of teaching is good or outstanding. Teachers have the highest expectations and plan lessons well to extend students' knowledge and understanding rapidly.'

Uffculme School (Secondary)

Whether you have chosen to provide a physical lesson plan or not, remember that the inspectors want to see a well-planned lesson that is moving students forward in their learning. Make sure you show this off to the students and the inspectors. Allow the students to see the learning journey that they are embarking upon so that they can articulate it and work in a focused way towards the desired endgame.

'Teachers continually assess the success of their teaching and alter what they are doing to help those finding the learning too challenging or moving on more rapidly for those who have quickly grasped the idea.'

Digby The Tedder Primary School (Primary)

You have a whole plethora of students sitting in front of you today. The differentiation that you have planned into your lesson and the knowledge you have of those students is so important. Keep checking that you have all your students where they need to be in the lesson and intervene as soon as you see someone who needs to be pulled back in.

Part 4

Afterwards

Overview

Once the visitors have left the building and the school is yours once again, there are a number of things that usually happen. The first is that the staff have a glass of something cold to congratulate themselves on getting through the inspection. Well deserved and not to be underestimated! While staff wind down and leave the site for the day your school's senior team will be meeting with Ofsted, the governors and then often meeting as a group to discuss the preliminary judgement that was given. The judgement given before the inspectors leave the site is always subject to change. The whole staff discussion around the inspection is often not had until the next day.

The headteacher will receive the draft report from the lead inspector and has a chance to make any comments they deem important. At this stage the actual report is still confidential. The final report will have an overall grade for the school: 1 is classified as outstanding, 2 as good, 3 is requires improvement and 4 is inadequate. There will be different approaches that Ofsted will take in the future with regards to your school as a result of this grading. The school will not receive the formal report straight away but once it does there will undoubtably be things to celebrate and others to work on. Most schools do well during an inspection but if your school's overall effectiveness is judged as inadequate then the inspectors will have to decide whether it requires 'serious weakness' or 'special measures'. The school will then be in a difficult but essential position of moving forward with support and guidance. Detailed information for these categories are available on the Ofsted website.

Your school will receive the inspection report no longer than 15 days after the inspection. Your school will be invited to fill in a post inspection survey. It will be up to your individual school how they share the results of the inspection with the students. Once your school receives the report they have five working days to send the report to parents and carers. Once this time is up the report will be available to the public on Ofsted's website.

This final section aims to give you the tools to reflect and learn from feedback following the inspection and guide you towards continuing your own improvement. The inspection is now over and you are left probably shell-shocked and reeling from the whole experience. Whatever the result there are things to celebrate and there are lessons to learn from. Now is the time to come together, reflect and plan your next steps. The inspection team are gone and staff are left to look over the report and feedback given. It is a time for development and discussion all round. You have all done well and you should celebrate while also being honest with yourselves and supporting those that need it.

I have included some guiding ideas on what you could focus on personally, with your team and as a whole school. After an inspection you are all tired and feeling the strain so these guidelines aim to help you form useful discussion and developmental reflection in order to regroup and refocus.

I have also included some possible next steps and future plans for once the dust has settled and discussions are over and done with and the time for action begins.

43

Personal reflections

"The road to success is not a path you find but a trail you blaze."

Robert Brault

Taking time to reflect on the areas you feel you could have done better in is just as important as the celebration that should so rightly be had in terms of what went well for you personally. However it is also important to remember not to take advice personally. Feedback is professional in this context and not personal. There are inevitable elements of your personality that are interwoven with your teaching practice, but it is not you that they are praising or criticising. Remember, it is the practice of teaching itself and how you could improve it that they are advising you on. You must detach the two to a degree in order to effectively move forward with the advice in mind.

Next steps

- **Ofsted feedback**: If you were lucky enough to be seen during the inspection then it is a good idea to look/think over the feedback you were given. I am not being sarcastic here, it really is a good thing if you are seen in the inspection. The inspectors are completely impartial and are coming in to look at you as a teacher with no preconceptions about you as a person or anything that has gone before. It can be a really useful process to go through. Ofsted will not grade you as a teacher or your lesson, and the feedback cannot be used for performance management purposes so take it for want it is – genuine feedback and professional guidance. There will always be areas that could have been improved upon and these should be seriously looked into. Take time to look over your lesson observation documents, think through your lesson and really take the time to consider how it went.

- **Support staff feedback**: You could also get some feedback on what went well from your teaching assistant – they often have a unique perspective and know whether the lessons you were teaching during the inspection are truly reflective of you as a teacher.

- **Student feedback**: Students are a great resource for feedback too. You could hold an open class discussion and ask what they feel went well or ask them to fill out a private written questionnaire if you feel you will get more from your class that way. It may surprise you what the students feel went well from their perspective. Often teachers are not openly proud of what they do well and there will be things that you can officially celebrate and will have no choice but to recognise as good practice on your part from the feedback.

- **Your thoughts**: Take some time to consider how you personally dealt with the whole inspection process in general. Did you handle some elements much better than you thought you would have done? Did you find the time to help another colleague in need? Were you happy with how you conveyed yourself in a meeting or interview? Make sure you look at the strengths you displayed during the inspection and give yourself credit. Equally, did you deal with any particular element of the inspection particularly badly? If so then don't brush over it, why didn't that go so well and can you think of how you could have approached that situation differently? Did you find yourself getting short with any staff or students at any point and if so what caused this? Making a plan for how you can better deal with the stress that naturally comes with caring about doing well is a healthy and essential process.

- **Team feedback:** Spending some time together as a team is a great way to wind down from the inspection process and share experiences. There will be some people within your team who were seen and had strengths highlighted so celebrations are in order. Your team's success is your success too. Spend time discussing observations, meetings or interviews that were experienced and what went well within those. Sharing success stories and how the inspection was made positive by some or all is empowering and developmental for all involved. Make sure you have an honest conversation about those things you knew you might be picked up on as a team as well as those things that came as a surprise and what part you feel you played in that. This is an opportunity for improvement and should be treated as such. If there is a particular member of the team that had a difficult time during the inspection then they will need your support to pick themselves back up and keep on improving. It is a team effort. Avoid blaming members of the team or gossiping about outcomes of the inspection. It is a tough thing to receive criticism and to use it to move forward positively; the more you group together and help each other the quicker improvements can be made.

Looking to the future

Make some plans for the future. Take on board all the things that you have experienced, talked about and reflected upon and think about how you personally want to move forward. Think of ways you can work even better with your support staff. Perhaps allowing them to lead parts of lessons, work with their personal strengths in class more, involving them in the planning process earlier. Make some plans to buddy up with people in your team and work on areas they did well in that you feel you could have done better in. Think of how the students responded to the inspection and your lesson and, if necessary, consider ways that you can help them not feel the impact of an inspection as much next time.

44

Whole school reflections

"Success is not final, failure is not fatal: it is the courage to continue that counts."

Winston Churchill

The job of moving forward is that of the whole school. The period following an Ofsted inspection is a time for everyone to pull together and for the whole school to work as one to take steps to sustain or create a better future for the students and staff who work there. It is vital that you work together at this stage. Bring what you have learnt about your and your team's strengths and weaknesses honestly to the table and plan as a whole. It is a time to listen to how everyone else did and felt during the process, what they learnt, enjoyed and regretted.

Things that were highlighted as areas for improvement should not come as a surprise, they should be things that were already being worked on. If there are any surprises look at the issues that were raised honestly and find solutions for those issues moving forward. This process is not for Ofsted, it is for everyone. Ofsted provide the feedback; we create the climate.

Next steps

- **Whole school debrief:** There will undoubtably be time given over in whole staff meetings to discussion of the inspection process and the things that went well over the course of the entire inspection. If you noticed someone doing well, something that was a strength or had any positive feedback from inspectors then share it with the staff. This is not boasting, we work hard and anyone or anything that is recognised as good practice should be focused on and appreciated. Sharing team reflections on the inspection process and how they coped well is a very useful process too.

- **Expert teachers**: Use the feedback from the Ofsted report along with your own knowledge of yourself or your team to form a group of 'expert teachers' who can lead on the areas they have been recognised as having good practice within. This shows an appreciation of strengths as well as giving an opportunity to develop others through sharing of good practice.

- **Project teams**: There will be key areas that Ofsted highlight as a whole school focus to improve on. These areas could be taken on as projects by a few key members of staff. Give meeting time over to project group meetings to action plan and implement ideas to improve these areas across the school. This is a great way for staff to get working collaboratively and an opportunity to really improve practice across the school.

- **In-house buddies:** There may well be areas of the school that you could help one another improve. Look at an area of improvement that was suggested for yourself or your team and see if there is a member of staff or team that were highlighted as doing this well and buddy up. Sometimes the help you need is right there on your doorstep all the time. Buddy people up and get them working collaboratively to develop one another.

- **Community sharing:** Making sure that a clear and accurate sharing of the strengths that were noted within the school and teams within the school with the families and community around the school is an important action. Teams will have reflected in depth on the strengths and this should be clearly explained and celebrated with all. Parents and the wider community rarely have insight into what really goes on in school, bar national press which can be very misleading indeed. Make sure your school takes charge of representing itself as it should.

- **Local school links**: Once the report has been digested and the positives pulled out and discussed, it is a great idea to open the school up to sharing this good practice with other local schools. Teaming up staff members across schools has so many benefits in terms of staff development and will allow your staff's strengths to be further embeded. Teaching others about what you do well helps you understand better *how* you do it well.

- **Local talent**: If there really is any area that is lacking within the school and there is not an appropriate staff member to lead on improvement in that area, then looking to local schools is a great next step. Look at the Ofsted report and exam results of schools in the local area and build links with them. Get staff out visiting for the day to see how they do things differently or set up shared CPD events to get the schools working together on projects.

Looking to the future:

Make sure you work with your line manager to put in place a clear and simple improvement plan for yourself, and be aware for those put in place for your team and your school. Know those plans well and base everything you do around them. Yes, Ofsted will come once again to your school in the future and the result of the inspection report will dictate how soon and how often they arrive at your gate. Don't let this rule your thoughts though. Remember any improvements you are making, however hard, as an individual or a school are for the good of the students and staff in the school. There will be difficult times and times for celebration, as there always is. Enjoy the ride with confidence that you are planning for a better future.

45

Reading the report

"Progress is impossible without change, and those who cannot change their minds cannot change anything."

George Bernard Shaw

Whatever the final result is in the end, there will always be some great successes to celebrate within the school. It is so important to make time to focus and build upon these. Certain departments, groups of staff or elements of how the school is run may well be flagged as good practice and this is a great achievement for all of those involved. If it is your team, or indeed you, that have been mentioned as a strength in the school then really do acknowledge that and take the time to reflect on how you or your team got to the stage where an external agency were able to see all the hard work and dedication that has gone on. The inspectors rarely have time to see all the good practice that goes on in a school during an inspection so there may well be an area or two where you know there are great things going on that have not been noted in the report – don't feel downhearted about this or feel that is is not as good as you thought. The inspectors simply cannot see everything in the school. There will be the informal feedback that has been received over the course of the inspection that can be mulled over as well as the official report that will be circulated once it is complete; both should be discussed and appreciated for the strengths that it has shown in your own practice, the team's and the school's as a whole.

Remember that you know your own teaching, team and school best. There will be elements that are picked up by the inspection team that need improvement because we all are imperfect and have areas that we should be working on. There may also be some surprises that come up in terms of areas that have been mentioned as in need of improvement. It can be difficult not to get defensive in response to criticism, even if it is constructive, but this is something you must battle. It is a time for self and group reflection. It is a time to be honest with yourselves and look openly at the areas that have been stated as areas still to work on as a school. We learn the most from our failures and downfalls if we grab them with both hands and work on them until we are happy with them. It may also be a time to think about how you show your strengths. Was it that you were unable to enable the inspectors to see what you feel is a strength – how can you change this in the future? Use weaknesses as a springboard for rapid improvements rather than a battering ram.

Next steps

- **Report breakdown**: Make sure you are fully aware of the strengths that have been highlighted within the school. Take the report to your team and highlight all the positives that were mentioned and discuss them as a team. It is important that everyone knows the things that should be celebrated across the school. Are there any strengths that you feel might have been missed out by the inspection team? If so make sure SLT are aware of these thoughts so that they can consider this. Taking time to highlight all of the areas of improvement within the report is a really important process. Extract them from the report and look seriously at a clear and practical action plan to improve upon them. Make sure everything that is done towards improvement is shared and documented so that there is a clear move from area for improvement to area of strength. Everyone working together and sharing steps of success along the way to better practice is uplifting and something that can be looked forward to.
- **Areas for improvement**: SLT will spend a lot of time going over the inspection report and then sharing this information with the wider school. It is important to have open and honest discussions around the recommendations that have been put forward as areas for improvement. Again, be sensitive to colleagues and teams that may have taken the inspection hard or had a significant

mention as an area to improve and rally around them to support. The school is a team and working together at a time like this will strengthen the whole structure.

Looking to the future

Know the areas for improvement in your Ofsted report and absolutely do your part to work toward the necessary improvements. But also ensure that you keep doing the things you do well and challenging yourself with new and exciting things in your practice. Be mindful not to become obsessed with THE OFSTED REPORT. It is a great tool so use it but don't become immersed in it. Keep the focus on improving learning and enabling your students to progress, and making the school you work in a place where staff and students want to be – that is the most important job you have.

References

Below are the references to the quotes taken from The framework of school inspection, School inspection handbook and Ofsted school reports. They are listed in the order they appear in the 'Inspection connection' boxes (parts 1–2) or 'What Ofsted said' sections (Part 3).

Chapter 1, page 5
School inspection handbook, 2015, page 61

Chapter 2, page 13
Ofsted, *The framework for school inspection*, 2015, page 14
Ofsted, *School inspection handbook*, 2015, page 61
Ofsted, *School inspection handbook*, 2015, page 41

Chapter 3, page 17
Ofsted, *School inspection handbook*, 2015, page 43
Ofsted, *School inspection handbook*, 2015, page 43

Chapter 4, page 21
Ofsted, *School inspection handbook*, 2015, page 53

Chapter 5, page 25
Ofsted, *School inspection handbook*, 2015, page 43

Chapter 6, page 30
Ofsted, *School inspection handbook*, 2015, page 57

Chapter 7, page37
Ofsted, *School inspection handbook*, 2015, page 41
Ofsted, *School inspection handbook*, 2015, page 40
Ofsted, *School inspection handbook*, 2015, page 41

Chapter 9, page 47
Ofsted, *School inspection handbook*, 2015, page 16
Ofsted, *School inspection handbook*, 2015, page 43
Ofsted, *School inspection handbook*, 2015, page 65

Chapter 10, page 52
Ofsted, *The framework for school inspection*, 2015, page 10
Ofsted, *School inspection handbook*, 2015, page 58
Ofsted, *School inspection handbook*, 2015, page 60

Chapter 11, page 59
Ofsted, *School inspection handbook*, 2015, page 58
Ofsted, *School inspection handbook*, 2015, page 16

Chapter 12, 64
Ofsted, *School inspection handbook*, 2015, page 49
Ofsted, *School inspection handbook*, 2015, page 55

Chapter 13, page 69
Ofsted, *School inspection handbook*, 2015, page 38
Ofsted, *School inspection handbook*, 2015, page 61
Ofsted, *School inspection handbook*, 2015, page 71

Chapter 14, page 73
Ofsted, *School inspection handbook*, 2015, page 29
Ofsted, *School inspection handbook*, 2015, page 38

Chapter 15, page 78
Ofsted, *School inspection handbook*, 2015, page 61
Ofsted, *School inspection handbook*, 2015, page 43

Chapter 16, page 84
Ofsted, *School inspection handbook*, 2015, page 71
Ofsted, *School inspection handbook*, 2015, page 75
Ofsted, *School inspection handbook*, 2015, page 22

Chapter 17, page 89
Ofsted, *The framework for school inspection*, 2015, page 14
Ofsted, *School inspection handbook*, 2015, page 71
Ofsted, *School inspection handbook*, 2015, page 52

Chapter 18, page 94
Ofsted, *School inspection handbook*, 2015, page 24

Chapter 19, 99
Ofsted, *The framework for school inspection*, 2015, page 14
Ofsted, *School inspection handbook*, 2015, page 52

Chapter 21, page 110
Ofsted, *School inspection handbook*, 2015, page 16
Ofsted, *School inspection handbook*, 2015, page 59
Ofsted, *School inspection handbook*, 2015, page 17

Chapter 22, page 115
Ofsted, *School inspection handbook*, 2015, page 43
Ofsted, *School inspection handbook*, 2015, page 61

Chapter 23, page 119
Ofsted, *The framework for school inspection*, 2015, page 10

Chapter 24, page 123
Ofsted, *School inspection handbook*, 2015, page 61

Chapter 25, page 125
Ofsted, *School inspection handbook*, 2015, page 58
Ofsted, *School inspection handbook*, 2015, page 59

Chapter 26, page 129
Ofsted, *The framework for school inspection*, 2015, page 14

Chapter 27, page 133
Ofsted, *School inspection handbook*, 2015, page 49

Chapter 28, page 137
Ofsted, *School inspection handbook*, 2015, page 61

Chapter 29, page 142
Ofsted, *School inspection handbook*, 2015, page 53

Chapter 30, page 147
Ofsted, *School inspection handbook*, 2015, page 24

Chapter 31, page 149
Ofsted, *School inspection handbook*, 2015, page 41

Chapter 32, page 153
Ofsted, *School inspection handbook*, 2015, page 53
Ofsted, *School inspection handbook*, 2015, page 58
Ofsted, *School inspection handbook*, 2015, page 61

Chapter 34, page 162
Ofsted, *School report: The Sacred Heart Language College*, 2014, page 1
Ofsted, *School report: Kielder Community First School and Little Squirrels
    Nursery*, 2014, page 1

Chapter 35, page 165
Ofsted, *School report: Highlands School*, 2014, page 1
Ofsted, *School report: Chorlton CofE Primary School*, 2014, page 1

Chapter 36, page 171
Ofsted, *School report: Outwood Academy Portland*, 2014, page 1
Ofsted, *School report: Elmore Green Primary School*, 2014, page 1

Chapter 37, page 174
Ofsted: *School report: The Westgate School*, 2014, page 1
Ofsted: *School report: Warmsworth Primary School, page 1*

Chapter 38, page 178
Ofsted: *School report: John Taylor High School*, 2014, page 1
Ofsted: *School report: St Paul's CofE Primary School*, 2014, page 1

Chapter 39, page 182
Ofsted: *School report: Harris Academy Greenwich*, 2014, page 1
Ofsted: *School report: Acresfield Community Primary School*, 2014, page 1

Chapter 40, page 185
Ofsted: *School report: Sirius Academy*, 2014, page 1
Ofsted: *School report: Curry Mallet Church of England Voluntary Controlled
    Primary School*, 2014, page 1

Chapter 41, page 188
Ofsted: *School report: St Olave's and St Saviour's Grammar School*, 2014, page 1
Ofsted: *School report: Stallingborough CofE Primary School*, 2014, page 1

Chapter 42, page 192
Ofsted: *School report: Ufculme School*, 2014, page 1
Ofsted: *School report: Digby The Tedder Primary School*, 2014, page 1

The spoken word quotes have been checked and verified to the best of the publisher's ability. If any quote has been misattributed or misquoted or any right has been omitted the Publishers offer their apologies and will rectify any error in subsequent editions following notification in writing by the copyright holder.

Index